What Others are Saying About

"Engaging in this study will delight your soul and clarify your purpose each day. What a glorious thought that God wants to praise *us*! I deeply appreciate the simple truths—grounded in Scripture—that Dwayne Moore has crafted into a daily tool for individuals or groups to immerse themselves in. This study is a gift to the kingdom!"

Nancy Beach • Champion for the Arts, Willow Creek Association

"This book, *Heaven's Praise*, is bedrock! Dwayne Moore lays a solid foundation for what it means to live an authentic Christian life that springs from the inside out. It is clear, cogent, and concise, providing readers with plenty of airspace so they are able to breath in what the Spirit of God is revealing to them. It begins at the heart of the matter: our intimacy with God and our motivation to bring him joy. Everything else flows from there. It is easy to follow, practical, and life-shaping. It is a great book for those who are just starting their journey with Jesus, as well as those who might get distracted along the way."

Stan Inouye • President and Founder, Iwa

"Worship is not what we do but *who we are*. To me, this describes Dwayne Moore. The principles of this book have been birthed out of a lifestyle of worship he has lived. Such faithfulness as Dwayne's will surely garner some praise from heaven one day. I truly believe your life will be impacted as these teachings challenge you to be that 'living worship' to Jesus as well."

Rusty Nelson • Lead Pastor, The Rock Family Worship Center, Huntsville, Alabama

"Every Christian longs to hear at the end of life's journey: 'Well done, good and faithful servant!' But do we understand the implications of these words in the here and now? *Heaven's Praise* explores the extraordinary notion that one day we will be the recipients of God's praise. This just might be the insight that gives weary modern Christians the fuel we need to finish the race. Highly recommended!"

Brett C. Blair • President/CEO, ChristianGlobe Network

"*Heaven's Praise* provokes the mind and the spirit and should lead any serious Christian to new heights of service....Intending to lead the reader to understand how heaven praises Christians, Moore succeeds in leading Christians to greater praise of God. I hope many people will go through this study. I think it will inspire all of us to better Christian living."

Dr. Robert Chambers • Johnson Bible College, Knoxville, Tennessee

"Imagine the most thrilling moment of your life. Now, imagine super-multiplying that excitement, wonder, and affirmation. That's what it could be like when you find yourself experiencing *Heaven's Praise*. Ready? Enjoy!"

Bill and Nancie Carmichael • Authors, *Surviving One Bad Year: 7 Spiritual Strategies to Lead You to a New Beginning*

"This is an excellent Bible study I'm glad to recommend to pastors and churches. This study builds on the solid premise of Matthew 25, encouraging each and every Christian to seek the words 'Well done, good and faithful servant' when all else has been said and done."

Dr. Amos Smith • Author and Pastor

"*Heaven's Praise* is a refreshing study. It embraces the right questions that challenge our preconceived culture-tainted or religion-altered notions. It also embraces the God-given biblical wisdom we all should be moving toward. And if that weren't enough, Dwayne is pretty funny, too!"

Jason Anderson • Executive Pastor, The Living Word, Mesa, Arizona

"*Heaven's Praise* is a dynamic book that will impact your spiritual walk in a powerful fashion. My advice: Read and apply. The results will be eternal."

Pat Williams • Senior Vice President, Orlando Magic

"In *Heaven's Praise,* my friend Dwayne Moore offers an engaging and inspiring study to revitalize your walk in Christ….Each chapter is filled with biblical insights to boldly challenge readers to aim right and act right, stay right and die right, and to finish well as we hear our Savior's words, 'Well done, good and faithful servant.' *Heaven's Praise* is a compelling book for all in ministry to learn how to pursue the call of God in Jesus Christ."

Branon Dempsey • CEO & Training Director, Worship Team Training

"So many Christians suffer from what I would call 'low Christ-esteem.' They simply don't know or understand how precious they are to God. In *Heaven's Praise,* Dwayne Moore gives us an invitation to truly know God as 'Father' and to learn to listen and follow the direction He sets for our lives….This book is a valuable guide for any Christian seeking to know God and walk in His ways."

Craig von Buseck • Ministries Director, CBN.com

"Don't we all long to hear, 'Well done' from our Heavenly Father? Dwayne Moore's book addresses one of your deepest yearnings. If you enjoyed Dwayne's first book, *Pure Praise,* you'll love *Heaven's Praise.*"

Rory Noland • Heart of the Artist Ministries

"It is one of the privileges of my life to get to serve alongside Dwayne Moore as his pastor and friend. I can tell you that *Heaven's Praise: Hearing God Say "Well Done"* is not just a book he's written—it's the passion of his life. This book is challenging me to live a life of greater obedience to the Lord, and I look forward to how God is going to use it in our church. Thank you, Dwayne, for sharing your heart. I know you long to hear your Father say it to you one day, but let me say it now about *Heaven's Praise*...well done."

Dr. Randy Norris • Pastor, The Church at Ross Station, Birmingham, Alabama

A 6-WEEK BIBLE STUDY

HEAVEN'S PRAISE

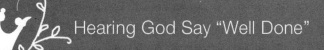

Hearing God Say "Well Done"

DWAYNE MOORE

Loveland, Colorado
group.com

Group resources actually work!

This Group resource incorporates our R.E.A.L. approach to ministry. It reinforces a growing friendship with Jesus, encourages long-term learning, and results in life transformation, because it's

Relational
Learner-to-learner interaction enhances learning and builds Christian friendships.

Experiential
What learners experience through discussion and action sticks with them up to 9 times longer than what they simply hear or read.

Applicable
The aim of Christian education is to equip learners to be both hearers and doers of God's Word.

Learner-based
Learners understand and retain more when the learning process takes into consideration how they learn best.

HEAVEN'S PRAISE

Hearing God Say "Well Done"

DWAYNE MOORE

Copyright © 2011 Dwayne Moore

Visit our website: **group.com**

Credits

Editor: Carl Simmons	Cover Art Director: Paul Povolni
Chief Creative Officer: Joani Schultz	Book Designer: Jean Bruns
Executive Editor: Becki Manni	Print Production Artist: Paragon Prepress
Copy Editor: Alison Imbriaco	Illustrator: Wes Comer/Frontlines Creative

Unless otherwise noted, Scriptures taken from the THE HOLY BIBLE, NEW INTERNATIONAL VERSION®, NIV® Copyright © 1973, 1978, 1984, 2010 by Biblica, Inc.™ Used by permission. All rights reserved worldwide.

Library of Congress Cataloging-in-Publication Data
Moore, Dwayne.
    Heaven's praise : hearing God say "well done" / Dwayne Moore.
      p. cm.
    Includes bibliographical references.
    ISBN 978-0-7644-4708-2 (pbk.)
    1. Talents (Parable) I. Title.
    BT378.T3M66 2011
    226.8—dc22
                2011001082

10 9 8 7 6 5 4 3 2 1   20 19 18 17 16 15 14 13 12 11

Printed in the United States of America.

C●NTENTS

Introduction .6

Week One: Think Right 8

    Daily Readings   8
    Small-Group Session   30

Week Two: Aim Right 34

    Daily Readings   34
    Small-Group Session   56

Week Three: Act Right 60

    Daily Readings   60
    Small-Group Session   82

Week Four: Stay Right 86

    Daily Readings   86
    Small-Group Session 108

Week Five: End Right 112

    Daily Readings   112
    Small-Group Session 136

Week Six: Win Right 140

    Daily Readings   140
    Small-Group Session 164

INTRODUCTION

As I was writing my first book, *Pure Praise: A Heart-Focused Bible Study on Worship* (Group), I came across a profound truth I had never seen or heard before. I still remember where I was when it first came to me—I was driving down the road, thinking how good I feel when I get to tell my kids how great they are. I thought, "I wonder if God ever wishes he could brag on his children." And then it hit me, "He plans to! One day, he's going to tell as many as he can, 'Well done!' "

I've mulled over this idea for more than two years now. It has been so exhilarating and fresh to me that it has utterly captivated my imagination. Could it be true? Does praise really work both ways? I know the Bible says again and again that we should praise God and tell him how wonderful and majestic he is, but might the God of the universe, who dwells on the heavenly throne far above this world, actually desire to praise *us*? Might there be a time I could receive accolades from my awesome Creator? I believe the answer is a resounding "Yes!"

Over the next six weeks, I believe you'll discover that God indeed loves and longs to praise his children. He looks forward to that time when he can say to us, "Well done, good and faithful servant!" (Matthew 25:21). As we explore Jesus' parable of the three servants in Matthew 25, you'll discover how to live a well-invested life of praise on this earth. If we carefully and humbly follow Jesus' teachings, God will almost certainly reciprocate with praise of his own.

This approach is summed up in a simple poem I call "The Servant's Creed." We'll refer to it often throughout our study, as it will act as our guide from week to week. Don't be surprised if, by the conclusion of the study, you have this poem memorized and internalized. That's one of my goals for you, in fact. Read it aloud right now.

THE SERVANT'S CREED

I yearn to know my Lord
Above all fortune and all fame.

To yield to him and love him more,
Then that must be my aim.

In serving Christ through serving men,
His praise I will proclaim.

By grace through faith I press to win
The prize and lift his name.

So when before my Lord I come,
Then I can hear him say:

"Well done, my good and faithful one;
You made the most of what I gave."

How You'll Do It

Each week contains five devotional lessons that reinforce a life goal for that week. You'll be asked to open and read the Bible and discover for yourself the truths being presented. I encourage you to read one lesson each day in a quiet place where you can consistently get alone with the Lord. Then take the time to use the journal space at the end of each lesson. You're much more likely to remember and apply what you're learning if you put it in writing.

There's nothing more vital and rewarding than a growing, passionate relationship with Jesus. In the segments at the end of each daily reading, "My Daily Response" and "My Daily Meditation," you'll focus your thoughts and prayers toward developing each of the life-transforming ideas and disciplines explored in the lesson.

At the end of each week's reading, you'll also find a weekly small-group session. Each session takes about an hour and includes questions and experiences that are fun, hard-hitting, or both. As you and your group dig deeper and push one another forward, your relationships with each other—and Jesus—will grow that much deeper. If you're leading these sessions, be sure to take a little time to read and familiarize yourself with them so you can lead in a natural, spontaneous way. Even if you don't have a small group and can't do the group activities, you can still take advantage of some great questions that will help you process what you learned during the week.

To help you fully grasp each week's teaching, I've also recorded weekly teaching videos. These video segments and other helpful resources are available at www.NextLevelWorship.com.

Ultimately, the goal of this study is for you to cultivate a life of personal prayer, more powerful praise and service to God, and more passionate pressing toward the prize of Jesus. I pray that, as you travel through this book, you'll fall head over heels in love with the Word of God, with the knowledge that Jesus is coming back for us, and most of all with Jesus himself.

May our precious Savior and King open the eyes of your heart as you go through this study. With his help and only by his grace, may we desire to honor and serve our Lord all the days and hours we have left on this earth, so that you and I may one day hear him say, "Well done!"

Longing to see him,
Dwayne Moore

THINK RIGHT

Praise From Heaven

Rewards await God's children. And God desires to praise us for our work on earth.

How did you feel as you read those statements? Uncomfortable? Did you cringe just a bit? Or did you just gloss over them, thinking, "Why bother focusing on something I don't deserve and can't be reasonably sure I'll obtain?"

If so, you're not alone.

It seems most Christians would rather occupy their thoughts with immediate pressing matters than look ahead to potential rewards in the "sweet by and by." It's almost as though they've resigned themselves to walking through this life the best they know how and hoping everything works out with God in the end. Many Christians feel completely unworthy and quite unlikely to get Jesus' stamp of ultimate approval: those famous words, "Well done, good and faithful servant!"

But it should be our life's goal to hear those words. Through Jesus' blood and power, we are made worthy and able to do what he's called us to do. We shouldn't feel guilty about wanting Jesus to commend us for the time we've invested on earth. In fact, we should try to do whatever it takes to someday receive his praise—not so much for our own benefit, but because our precious Lord *deserves* the opportunity to give us that reward.

Stop now and read the parable of the three servants in Matthew 25:14-30. Notice how the master commended the two loyal servants for investing the money he entrusted to them, but condemned the wicked and lazy one.

As you read, did you get the sense the master enjoyed commending his faithful servants? Put yourself in that master's place. How would *you* feel?

Our Lord and Master, Jesus Christ, both desires and deserves the chance to shower us with praise for a job well done. He paid a tremendous price for us, and we owe him that joy. He invested himself in us; he died, rose from the dead, and at this very moment is interceding for us before his Father. He is cheering us on, and he wants us to win—and win big!

Was there someone in your life who poured time, energy, and resources into helping you accomplish a dream? Perhaps it was your parents, grandparents, or simply a good friend who really wanted you to succeed. Let's say you have a gift for playing baseball or maybe a talent for playing the violin. That person would have invested money in your lessons or come to all your games and never quit encouraging and cheering you on as you developed your abilities.

Imagine that at last the day comes when you have the opportunity to play in the World Series or premiere your virtuosic skills at a concert with a philharmonic orchestra. The crowd is on edge as you step up to the plate to bat or raise your bow to play. This is the moment you've dreamed of. And you don't disappoint. You play your heart out. The beautiful notes soar through the music hall. Or your hit goes flying over the outfield fence. The crowd goes wild. Everyone's on their feet, clapping and shouting.

But as you lower your violin and take your bow, or as you round the bases, you're not thinking about all those other people out there cheering for you. Your eyes scan the crowd for your mom or dad or friend who made all this possible, the one who sacrificed so much so you could have this moment. When your eyes meet, and you see the pure joy and pride on that person's face, no one else's applause and no one else's approval even compares.

That's how it is with God's praise of you and me: Nothing will bring more pleasure to us—or to *him*.

You see, striving for heaven's rewards doesn't mean we're being selfish or unappreciative. Heaven's praise isn't only for *our* benefit. Any crowns and praises we're given at the end of our journey ultimately bless our greatest supporter and friend, our Lord and Savior, Jesus. Every honor we might receive only serves to make *him* more glorious and reminds us again of his awesome grace shown to awful sinners.

Now, I realize that implying—much less declaring—that God would praise mere mortals seems strange, even blasphemous, to some. But according to *Websters' New World College Dictionary,* the verb form of *praise* means "to commend the worth of; express approval or admiration of." As a noun, praise means "commendation," "an expression of admiration." God is and always will be our most holy and awesome superior, before whom we will all ultimately bow and be judged. Saying that God will honor certain people with words of praise doesn't mean he'll give up any glory of his own or that he'll suddenly acknowledge anyone else as his equal. Rather, God will enthusiastically commend those who show outstanding and faithful service.

Rewards Aren't for Everyone

Now read 1 Corinthians 3:10-15. Which building materials do you think will survive, and what will the builder receive if he or she uses those materials? What do those materials look like in *our* lives?

While many people have a hard time accepting the idea that God will reward them, others assume that receiving rewards from God is automatic for all Christians. They think that as soon as they walk through the pearly gates, Jesus will be standing there with outstretched arms, saying "Well done" to everyone who enters. But this is far from the truth. Many works will burn and not stand the test of Christ's judgment.

Those of us who have placed our trust in Jesus will be allowed into heaven to have the eternal life we were promised (1 Corinthians 3:15). That's because salvation is based on faith, not works, and on God's grace, not our merit (Ephesians 2:8-9). Unfortunately and quite unnecessarily, however, not everyone will have the privilege of hearing Jesus speak precious words of approval to them.

While it's true that heavenly rewards are determined by how we invest our lives on earth, it never becomes about whether we deserve them or not. We don't deserve *heaven*, much less any special honors we might receive after we arrive! But because of God's mercy, every one of us has the invitation and opportunity to earn praise—and the *possibility* of being applauded by the King of kings himself!

Results May Vary—and That's OK

Go back to Matthew 25. Read verses 19-23 again. Compare the return on investment the two servants earned. Now compare the master's response to each servant. What's different? Or rather, what's not?

I'm so thankful God doesn't base his goodness to me on what someone else has accomplished, aren't you? I've sat in boardrooms and sales meetings when my sales numbers have been plastered right alongside the heavy hitters' numbers. I know how it feels to be compared to guys who have far more experience and skill than I have. Likewise, there will always be Christians who have more spiritual gifts, more opportunities, and thus more outward fruit in their Christian lives than we have. Fortunately, God is only concerned that you and I take what he's entrusted to us and make the most of it. If we do that, our heavenly "Boss" counts us as just as faithful and successful as the spiritual heavy hitters.

One note to my older readers: Perhaps you feel you've outlived your usefulness to the Master. Maybe you squandered some of your earlier years and think the time you have left is too little too late. "What could possibly come of investing my life for the Lord *now*?" you wonder. Remember the loaves and fishes that Jesus took and multiplied to feed thousands? (If not, read Matthew 14:13-21.) Never underestimate God's ability to take your "little" and turn it into "much." Your time on this earth may not be extensive, but oh, what God can do in the time you have!

Others reading this may feel that their past sins will disqualify them from ever hearing a "Well done" from Jesus. If you're one of those readers, please listen

to these words: "Because of the Lord's great love we are not consumed, for his compassions never fail. They are new every morning; great is your faithfulness" (Lamentations 3:22-23). God's compassion and mercy are new for you today. Trust that Jesus has cleansed you of your past. Don't dwell in it anymore! The old adage is true: Today is the first day of the rest of your life. And your life has incredible value to God. Go and invest it for him—in gratitude for how God has forgiven and restored you.

Every one of us should look at ourselves in the mirror and boldly speak these words: "I can hear the Lord say, 'Well done.'" We need to repeat them with enthusiasm and gratitude—all the while knowing that they are marvelously true! Let's decide right now to stay faithful to our calling and to invest our lives—every last ounce and minute of them—for Jesus. Let's lose our lives in Christ and settle for nothing less than one day receiving *heaven's praise…*

My Daily Response

Be still now, and listen to what God may be saying to you. What's your attitude been toward heavenly rewards? Do you think it's OK to want to hear Jesus say "Well done" to you? Or does wanting to hear those words make you feel selfish and self-serving? Honestly, do you believe you have a *chance* of hearing Jesus say "Well done"? Journal your responses below.

JOURNAL

Each day you'll be challenged to meditate on Scriptures and truths that relate to our study. The purpose of the meditation section is to help you cultivate a lifestyle of praise that can, in turn, culminate in accolades from your Master!

This week's focus will be on Romans 12:2. "Don't copy the behavior and customs of this world, but let God transform you into a new person by changing the way you think. Then you will learn to know God's will for you, which is good and pleasing and perfect" (New Living Translation). What does this verse teach you about the importance of thinking right? Journal your thoughts.

JOURNAL }

HEAVEN'S
PRAISE

What does it mean to "invest" our lives? How do we accomplish that?

Many believe we make the most of our lives when we're *successful*. Every day, people succeed in their jobs or with their families or in other relationships. We often hear of individuals who become overnight sensations or join the ranks of the independently wealthy. Not a week passes that someone doesn't graduate or get a promotion. Success in life is not unusual for many people. However, while many succeed *in* life, the unfortunate truth is that far fewer actually succeed *at* life.

Despite what we may have been told, life is, in reality, quite long. In fact, it is *eternally* long. The only thing short about our lives is the brief part we live on earth! The few years we have here are no longer than the dash between the dates that will one day be etched on our tombstones. King David wrote,

> All our days pass away under your wrath;
>   we finish our years with a moan.
> Our days may come to seventy years,
>   or eighty, if our strength endures;
> yet the best of them are but trouble and sorrow,
>   for they quickly pass, and we fly away.
>
> (Psalm 90:9-10)

Once our time on earth is finished, our spirits will live on. Who we are now will determine where and how we'll live for the rest of our eternal days. Perhaps that's why David went on to say in Psalm 90:12: "Teach us to number our days, that we may gain a heart of wisdom."

So let's reconsider how we measure success. People may garner great accomplishments during this life yet fail to prepare for life after death. And since our existence is eternal, these same seemingly "successful" people will ultimately fail at life itself. And failure in that regard is neither acceptable nor advisable.

The story of the rich man and Lazarus in Luke 16:19-34 is most likely a true story, rather than a parable, because Jesus called Lazarus by name.[1] Please read that story now. Note how successful the rich man was on earth compared with Lazarus. Which person would you say ultimately succeeded?

The hard fact is that we can't afford to fail at this God-given gift called life— and that we need to have the right definitions of *success* and *failure*. Listen to these sobering words from Jesus: "What good will it be for someone to gain the whole world, yet forfeit their soul? Or what can anyone give in exchange for their soul?" (Matthew 16:26). The only one who can judge whether our time on earth is truly successful is the Creator of life itself.

A Strategy for Success *at* Life

Throughout this study, we'll return to a six-part poem called "The Servant's Creed." Absorb it. Chew on it. By doing so, we'll give ourselves the greatest opportunity to hear Jesus say "Well done" to us when our time on earth is finished.

The Servant's Creed

Think right:
I yearn to know my Lord
Above all fortune and all fame.
Aim right:
To yield to him and love him more,
Then that must be my aim.
Act right:
In serving Christ through serving men,
His praise I will proclaim.
Stay right:
By grace through faith I press to win
The prize and lift his name.
End right:
So when before my Lord I come,
Then I can hear him say:
Win right:
"Well done, my good and faithful one;
You made the most of what I gave."

As we *think right* thoughts about God and ourselves, we are compelled to *aim right* at worshipping him completely. As we worship him from our hearts, we can quite naturally (*and* supernaturally) praise him before others as we outwardly *act right*. Through God's grace and power, we can *stay right,* remaining consistent and growing in our faith until our dying day. We will therefore *end right,* with peace and joy, knowing we kept the faith and finished well. And thus we will *win right,* or win "the prize," as the Apostle Paul put it in 1 Corinthians 9:24. And the prize Paul refers to is far better than anything we could ever hope to win on this earth, for it will last forever.

This approach to life won't help us win the lottery; it won't help us get rich quick. It's not some secret formula for climbing to the top of the corporate ladder or for finding that perfect mate. However, as we delve deeper into this simple plan over the next six weeks, what we'll find is real and lasting hope. We'll discover that

God has an incredible plan custom-designed for each of us, because God loves and values each of us. Forgiveness for our past and restoration for our future are ours for the taking. The life given to each of us has definite purpose and importance.

My prayer is that you'll discover how you can best invest your time here on earth and truly succeed at the *long* version of life.

A Successful Life Begins With Dying

Let's return to the parable of the three servants in Matthew 25:14-30. Read it now. This time, focus on the master's response to the unfaithful servant. Let's be honest—doesn't it seem a bit harsh? It certainly did to me. After all, the master in the parable clearly represents Jesus. And the Jesus I know and love gives second, third, and tenth chances when we let him down. So why would he cast someone into hell and eternal separation from him as punishment for failing to invest a bag of gold?

Here's my theory: I believe that the one bag of gold the unfaithful servant received represents the most basic and sacred gift of all. While some may have several gifts, God has entrusted to every one of us at least one—the gift of *life*. Therefore, we must be sure we invest it wisely. I love how a friend of mine puts it: "Life is not a video game that lets us put in a couple of coins and start over when we mess up. We've got one shot, and we'd better make it count."

Jesus said, "Unless a kernel of wheat falls to the ground and dies, it remains only a single seed. But if it dies, it produces many seeds" (John 12:24). If we're to make the most of this life we've been entrusted with, we must first *die* to our sin and ourselves. Jesus called the unfaithful servant "wicked," meaning he had never died to his own wants and his own way; his heart had never surrendered to the master's will.

Stop and ask yourself these questions: Have I completely surrendered my life to Jesus? *Every* part of my life? Have I asked Jesus to forgive me and cleanse me and come into my life?

Before you can even hope to hear Jesus say "Well done" one day, you must first be his child. If you haven't already, trust Jesus as your Savior right now. Don't put it off even for a moment. Invest your life by first allowing Christ to give you new life in him!

Here's the bottom line: We can't possibly *think* right until we *get* right. Our thoughts don't shape our hearts; our hearts shape our thoughts. And no matter how hard we may try, no matter how many good thoughts we muster, we simply can't change our hearts. Only God can fashion in you and me a clean heart. We must pray, as David did, "Create in me a pure heart, O God" (Psalm 51:10).

What's God saying to you right now about your ideas of success and failure? What hopes and dreams do you have? What excites you? What inspires you? Now think about this: Did some form of "serving Jesus and living only for him" show up anywhere in your answers? How have you measured success in the past? How might you need to change your "standard of measure"? Journal your thoughts.

JOURNAL }

My Daily Meditation

Jesus said he "did not come to be served, but to serve, and to give his life as a ransom for many" (Matthew 20:28). Think about how Jesus set the example of a servant. How might you be a success today by serving someone else? Draw a picture of it—literally—in the space below. (Don't worry; no one else is watching.) Then pray that God would shape your heart to that of a servant.

JOURNAL }

[1] Randy Alcorn, *Heaven* (Carol Stream, IL: Tyndale, 2004), 62

Life's Greatest Pursuit

When you think of the best things in life, what comes to mind? Money? Fame? Pleasure? Many in our society think of at least one of those things as worthy of their pursuit. Or perhaps, you think of isolation and separation from this world and a focus on purity in mind and body. According to the ascetics, contemplative living is man's greatest quest. Then there are the treasure hunters who invest years of their lives in the search for hidden and unknown riches. Others believe there are secret truths and wisdom in the universe that only the most faithful and determined will ever discover and know. And then there are the spiritualists, who speak often very generally or eclectically of "god" and spiritual things. They believe that their understanding of spiritual knowledge will somehow bring about harmony and happiness in their world and their own personal lives.

As passionately as people may pursue these goals, none of them qualifies as life's *greatest* pursuit. Instead all reflect our futile attempts to find life's purpose and goals apart from the Creator of life; they are a mere "chasing after the wind" (Ecclesiastes 4:4).

The Bible tells us that life's greatest pursuit is not about finding something or someone—it's about *being* found. Jesus said in John 15:16, "You did not choose me, but I chose you." Before the earth and the heavens were made, God had a plan and a purpose for us. In *The Voice* translation of the New Testament, Romans 8:29 says, "*From the distant past,* His eternal love reached into the future, and He chose those who would be conformed to the image of His Son."

Did you ever get separated from your parents or guardians when you were little? I remember the first time I got lost. I was in a large mall (to a four-year-old, it was huge!). I walked aimlessly. I had no idea where to go or what to do. I just knew I wanted my mommy and daddy! Fortunately, after some searching, they finally found me. Notice I didn't say *I* found *them.* I was helpless and desperate on my own. No matter how passionately I "pursued" my parents, I simply was not able to find them.

So it is with us and God. We are completely unable to find God or reach up to him, so he came down to us to meet us right where we are (hallelujah!).

However, once God initiates the relationship—once he "finds" us and we become his children—it's time to return the favor. We're to invest the rest of our lives in seeking *God,* getting to know him more and more intimately even as he continues to reveal himself to us.

The beginning of Jeremiah 29 is a letter the prophet wrote to the exiled priests and elders in Babylon. It's important to keep in mind that the people to whom this letter was addressed were Israelites, God's chosen people. God had already initiated the relationship. They already belonged to him.

Read Jeremiah 29:10-14. Notice in verse 13 what God expected the Israelites to do, what they were responsible to do to "find" him.

Now turn to Proverbs 2:1-6. Where does wisdom come from, and what should we be willing to do to have it? What will we ultimately find? And how do we get it?

God wants us to *know* him. Whatever the cost, we are to seek him with our whole heart. If we knew there was great treasure buried in our yard, we'd spare no expense and work our fingers to the bone to dig it up, wouldn't we? With the same amount of passion, we should search for the hidden treasure our awesome God has made available to us. And we can be assured that as we do he will make himself known!

A Game of Darts

Most people are familiar with the game of darts. It certainly seems simple enough to play: Just pick up a dart, and try to hit the bull's-eye. But as with most sports, being really good at darts requires skill and knowledge.

Let me ask a trick question: If a person wanted to become a champion dart thrower, what should that dart player set as the primary goal? Think carefully before you answer. Should the primary goal be to win? If the goal is to become a champion dart thrower, winning should *not* be the first consideration.

Obviously, winning is important. Nonetheless, the mere *will* to win is not sufficient to assure success. One can wish and think all day long about winning and still be no closer to conquering the game. I've played darts from time to time, and every time I played I really wanted to win. But to no one's surprise but my own, I can count on one hand the number of times I actually *have* won.

While winning is certainly the objective of the *game*, it shouldn't be the most important objective for the *player*. Instead, what the dart thrower needs to reach for and attain above all is *knowledge* of the game of darts and skill at throwing darts. Before the dart thrower can hope to play well, he or she must first know the game's rules and understand the special strategies involved. The more the player understands about how to play darts and especially about the board itself, the greater the chances the player will come out a winner in the end.

The same is true in this "game" called life. If we really want to win at life, there is something we must know—or rather, there is some*one* we must know. A deep knowledge and understanding of our Lord is absolutely necessary if we are to truly be successful in this life.

And this knowledge must get into our hearts, not just our heads. Divine knowledge—knowledge that comes *from* God and isn't just *about* God—changes

the way we live and behave. Peter Lord said, "The first basis of religion is that we really get to know God, so we can properly respond to him."[2]

Now, here's another trick question: Is the bull's-eye the best target if we want to win the game? If that's what you thought, then you're a novice like me! The fact is, we *shouldn't* aim for the bull's-eye. Professional players know to aim for the *triple 20*, which is located in the thin middle portion, roughly halfway between the outer wire and the central circle. Hitting it with all three darts gives a player a total of 180 points, the highest score possible in darts. Can you see why *knowledge* of the game is so important?

How much more vital is it for us to know what God has revealed about himself? We may think we know God. But only as we dig deep into his Word and invest time in his presence do we discover who God *really* is. We cannot win at life if we don't truly know the Lord and what he expects of us. I believe that's one reason Paul said, "I want to know Him *inside and out*. I want to experience the power of His resurrection. *I want to find myself deeper in the path of the Liberating King,* joined in His suffering, shaped by His death" (Philippians 3:10, *The Voice*).

My Daily Response

Write out Romans 12:2 in the space below. As you do, think about how Paul's counsel points us toward a deeper knowledge of God's "good, pleasing and perfect will."

As long as we are on this earth, we have the privilege—in fact, the tremendous need—to get to know the one and only God more and more. That's why "The Servant's Creed"—the poem and prayer upon which our study is structured—begins with these powerful words:

> *I yearn to know my Lord*
> *Above all fortune and all fame.*

Please read those words out loud several times. Make them your prayer before God right now.

JOURNAL

Carefully read Romans 11:33-36. The refrain of the hymn "One Day," by J. Wilbur Chapman, proclaims:

> "Living, He loved me; dying, He saved me;
> Buried, He carried my sins far away;
> Rising, He justified freely forever;
> One day He's coming—O glorious day!"

Take as much time as you need right now to dwell on that glorious day. Imagine Jesus breaking through the clouds to take his children home. Then pray. Let Jesus know you'll watch for him as you go through your day today.

JOURNAL

[2] Peter Lord, "We Are Righteous, Part 1," audio, www.DiscipleshipLibrary.com.

HEAVEN'S PRAISE

Our Relationship With the Father

You've no doubt heard the old saying, "You are what you eat." That may be true of our bodies, but when it comes to our minds, emotions, and spirits, we are what we *think*. And the most profound thoughts any human can have are thoughts about God. That is precisely why this study starts with an emphasis on thinking right. How we relate to God and how we believe he relates to us affects every facet of what we do and who we are. So we'd better get our thinking straight about God!

Let's look at three distinct yet common stances Christians take regarding their relationship with God:

1. He's the Boss; I'm the worker
2. He's the Teacher; I'm the student
3. He's the Father; I'm his child

Let's assume for a moment we think of God primarily as our boss. What does a boss expect of his employees? He expects them to produce, perform, work hard, and show results for their labor. But a boss's interest in workers is based on what they *do*, not who they are. Therefore, those who produce the most win the boss' approval. Those who lag behind and don't perform up to expectations are usually reprimanded or fired. In a business environment, a boss isn't motivated to love the people who work for him or her, and the boss's obligation toward those employees is limited.

I'm thankful that God's not primarily a boss, aren't you?

Now let's try God as teacher. What does a teacher expect of students? A teacher wants students to apply themselves to getting good grades and high test scores. A teacher's focus on students is limited by the classroom. While teachers often care deeply that students will be able to apply what they're learning and use what they learn to improve their lives, they are required to spend their days helping students "make the grade."

I'm very thankful that God is much more than a teacher, aren't you?

Please don't misunderstand me. I know there are many wonderful bosses and teachers who care deeply for the people they're responsible for and go far beyond the call of duty to get involved with their lives. But that's the point I want to make: Bosses and teachers who emulate Jesus have a unique quality about them that comes from another aspect of God—one which encompasses and supersedes all the others.

Father First

Please read 2 Corinthians 6:16-18. According to verse 18, what relationship does God long to have with us, his people?

The supreme revelation of God in the Bible is that he is first of all a Father and that he is the God and Father of our Lord Jesus Christ. John 1:14 tells us: "The Word became flesh and made his dwelling among us. We have seen his glory, the glory of the one and only Son, who came from the Father, full of grace and truth."

Did you catch those last words? The Father is full of grace and truth. God's love is unconditional. He wants us to be his children, so much so that he sent his one and only Son, Jesus, to die in our stead. "See what great love the Father has lavished on us, that we should be called children of God!" (1 John 3:1a).

As our heavenly Father, God *is* our boss, whom we are to obey and follow. But unlike human bosses, our Father wants only what's best for us. We don't have to perform and work hard to make him accept us. He loves us just as we are. He is pleased with us simply because we are his children. And when we do wrong, he doesn't get rid of us. Instead, he lovingly disciplines us to make us more like Jesus.

As our teacher, God the Father gently and patiently instructs us through the Holy Spirit. But God's purpose in teaching us is not so we'll ace some pop quiz. Rather, it's so we'll know how to live for his glory. And if we fail a test or if we're not as bright and quick to catch on as others, it doesn't mean we are less favored in God's sight. Every one of God's children is his favorite!

A relationship with a boss can be severed. As quickly as someone can hand you a termination slip, you are out the door, never to return. A relationship with a teacher can run its course and come to an end, and you may never see that teacher again. But a relationship with your Father—now that's permanent; that's forever. Read Jesus' powerful words, recorded in John 10:27-30, about our relationship with him and his Father. Then read them again. Let this phenomenal and freeing truth sink into your soul.

I am so incredibly thankful that the God of the Bible, the true and living God, is first and foremost my Father, aren't you?

A Down-to-Earth Example

My father passed away when I was only ten years old, but I was old enough to have some very fond memories of him. My dad was far from perfect, mind you—I'm not even sure he was a Christian—but he loved me. Of that I never had a doubt. I can't count how many times he let me fall asleep in his lap while his big arms wrapped around me and held me tight.

I remember the time I accidentally set off an entire pack of firecrackers inside our house! I had been playing with them in our living room just out of sight of my dad, who was watching TV and resting from a long day's work. I will never forget seeing him jump out of his chair and spring to life at the sound of those obnoxiously loud firecrackers hopping wildly across our hardwood floor! He did his best to kick the fiery pack out the front door, but most of the miniature bombs

HEAVEN'S PRAISE

had already exploded, leaving behind a room full of dark smoke and a mass of shredded paper and soot.

I still remember the look on his face when he turned to me. Boy, was he mad! At that moment, I saw my life flash before my eyes. And I was already imagining what choice words he might use on my tombstone! But instead, he slowly forced his body in the direction of his chair, sat down, and quietly looked toward the TV. I recall hurriedly cleaning up my mess and opening the front door wide to let out the smoke.

Then the most amazing thing happened. My dad motioned for me to once again climb into my most cherished and safe place. Instead of giving me the whipping I deserved, he simply held me again. He never said a word. I think he knew I'd learned my lesson and that what I really needed was to know he still loved and accepted me, despite my stupid and dangerous mistake!

When I think about how loving my earthly father was, I'm reminded of how much greater and more loving our heavenly Father is. Jesus said, "If you, then, though you are evil, know how to give good gifts to your children, how much more will your Father in heaven give good gifts to those who ask him!" (Matthew 7:11).

In the Beloved

Please read Luke 3:21-22. How much do you think God delighted in saying those words—and, for that matter, how much do you think Jesus delighted in *hearing* them?

Jesus lived thirty-three years—more than twelve thousand days—on this earth, yet he never sinned. He was truly the spotless, perfect Lamb of God. Not long before Jesus' death and just after Jesus was transfigured on the mountain, the Father repeated words he spoke at Jesus' baptism. "A bright cloud overshadowed them; and suddenly a voice came out of the cloud, saying, 'This is My beloved Son, in whom I am well pleased. Hear Him!'" (Matthew 17:5, NEW KING JAMES VERSION).

With the Father's words about his Son in mind, flip to Ephesians 1:1-6. Slowly savor Paul's words describing who *we* are in Jesus. The King James Bible puts Ephesians 1:6 this way: "To the praise of the glory of his grace, wherein he hath made us accepted in the beloved."

Now let's put this all together: How did the Father describe Jesus? He said Jesus is his beloved Son. And who are we "in," according to Ephesians 1:6? So if Jesus is accepted by God, and we are hidden in Jesus, guess what? We, too, are accepted by God the Father! If we've trusted Jesus as Savior, there's nothing more we can do to make ourselves more pleasing to or approved by our heavenly Father!

Before we can move forward in our study of heaven's praise—before we can even hope to hear Jesus say "Well done" one day—we *have to* understand and embrace this overarching truth: God is, first of all, our heavenly Father who loves us *unconditionally*.

How do you most often relate to God? Do you believe your ways of relating are healthy and proper? Do you ever wonder if you truly *are* pleasing to God? Or do you feel that God doesn't really like you and might, in fact, be mad at you about something?

Now step back and consider *this:* Perhaps you grew up with an earthly father who was cruel, unloving, distant, and maybe even abusive to you or to others in your family. If so, you may find it difficult—even painful—to think of God as your Father.

Stop right now and review Romans 12:2. Try to do it from memory first. Then consider this: What parts of your thinking does God need to transform? Please open your heart right now. Ask God to shine his perfect love and peace inside it. Trust God to reshape your feelings and attitudes about him as your perfect Father. Journal any thoughts and prayers.

JOURNAL

Read and meditate on Psalm 103. What attributes of the Father can you easily identify with and cultivate even further? Which attributes do you have a hard time accepting or understanding? Verbalize your answers to both of those questions to God right now.

Then thank God for what he's already revealed about himself to you, as well as those things you still find hard to grasp about God but that remain true. Ask God to help you not only say those things about him but also *see* them.

JOURNAL

HEAVEN'S
PRAISE

Our Relationship With the Son

We throw around the idea of relationships so often that when we try to associate the concept with Jesus, we almost don't do it justice. Far more than some shallow acquaintance or even a deep human bond, our relationship with Christ is above and beyond any other relationship we'll ever have. I love how a hymn from my childhood, "Trust and Obey" by John H. Sammis, puts it, "When we walk with the Lord in the light of his Word, what a glory he sheds on our way." Yet, even that poetic verse is a huge understatement. I don't believe words can adequately describe the light and life, the joy and peace, the hope and purpose, that Jesus brings to us.

When I said yes to Jesus as a six-year-old boy, I had no clue what I had gotten myself into. As I sit typing these words, my mind races back to that little wood-frame country church, when on a crisp Sunday morning in October, my world was literally turned downside up—all because Jesus came into my heart!

Jesus relates to his followers in many wonderful ways, not just one or two. And how I relate best to Jesus is probably somewhat different from how you tend to relate to him. Let's look at a few of those precious and powerful ways today. But let's start with the one title by which we all must know Jesus.

Our Savior

John the Baptist was having another wonderfully normal day baptizing folks down by the Jordan River in Bethany. Then he looked up and saw the most awesome sight, one he had somehow anticipated even when in his mother's womb—Jesus, in the distance, walking toward him. John had been sent from God to prepare the way for the One who was, at that very moment, approaching. What would John say? What would be the first words he would speak to welcome this King to earth?

Read John 1:29-31 now, and discover those words for yourself.

The most important role Jesus came to fulfill was that of Savior, the Lamb of God, who takes away our sin. The name *Jesus* literally means "The Lord saves." Jesus himself said, "For the Son of Man came to seek and to save the lost" (Luke 19:10). Only Jesus, by dying on the cross, could buy back the title deed to our souls that Satan had stolen. Only our Savior could open the way to God. Jesus plainly said, "I am the way and the truth and the life. No one comes to the Father except through me" (John 14:6).

Jesus called himself the "gate" (John 10:9). Before we met Jesus, we were standing on the outside, so to speak—lost, cold, alone, and without hope. But when we placed our faith and trust in Jesus, we came through the gate or door to the *inside,* where there is warmth in the love and fellowship of our loving Lord.

Before we go any further, stop and take some time to praise and thank your Savior, who took the penalty of your sin and gave you eternal life.

Once Jesus became our Savior, what amazing resources suddenly became available to us through our "inside" relationship with him! Imagine stepping into a huge mall at Christmastime—except everything you see, once you are inside, is *free*! Truly, we could spend a lifetime and not discover all the benefits available to us simply because Jesus is our Savior.

Our Shepherd

Another of my personal favorite ways to relate to Jesus is as my shepherd. Please read John 10:1-15. As you do, underline in your Bible, or jot down in the margin of this page, the benefits you see from being Jesus' sheep and having him as your shepherd.

Now read Psalm 23, one of the most beloved passages in the Bible. Again, note the many benefits David mentions in this psalm.

Verse 4 of Psalm 23 almost always seizes me and stops me in my tracks. Perhaps it's because I've peered into "the valley of the shadow of death," as it's called in the King James Bible, a time or two, as I've stood beside the caskets of close friends and family members. I've been comforted countless times by the rod of correction when I've gone astray, knowing in my heart that the Lord disciplines those he loves. I've been calmed and reassured by his staff of protection, knowing that the wolves and enemies would not devour me. What's more, my Shepherd has had to use that same staff to pull this sheep out of a few ditches I've fallen into during moments of carelessness and recklessness! Can you relate?

Our Source

Another favorite analogy of mine comes from John 15 where Jesus described himself as the vine and us as branches. This potent word picture is so loaded with benefits and application that we could spend an entire month of study on it and not exhaust all that can be drawn from it! Jesus is truly the source of our lives.

Suffice it to say that because Jesus is our vine into which we are solidly grafted, we have all the nutrients and provisions we will *ever* need to bear tons of fruit for his glory!

Our Sibling

This is a facet of our relationship with Jesus that's rarely talked about among most Christians. However, it's a fascinating and marvelous way we can relate to Jesus.

Matthew 12 tells us that while Jesus was talking to a crowd of people, his family came to see him. But rather than going out to meet them, Jesus pointed to his disciples and said, "Here are my mother and my brothers. For whoever

does the will of my Father in heaven is my brother and sister and mother" (Matthew 12: 49-50).

Romans 8:16-17 gives us a clearer picture of what Jesus meant: "The Spirit himself testifies with our Spirit that we are God's children. Now if we are children, then we are heirs—heirs of God and co-heirs with Christ." We have the same Father in heaven that Jesus has! Therefore, believe it or not, Jesus is also our big brother! All the resources and riches available to Jesus are also available to *us*. Let *that* sink in for a few minutes. Who needs the lottery when we've got the *Lord*!

Our Friend

As thrilling as it is to have Jesus as our big brother, he wants to take our relationship even further. He wants to have a close *friendship* with us. Proverbs 18:24 says, "One who has unreliable friends soon comes to ruin, but there is a friend who sticks closer than a brother." Jesus doesn't want to be—and *won't* be—just another one of our pals. He longs to be closer to us than we are with our own brothers and sisters.

I love how Jesus' friendship is not dependent on our social status or coolness factor. Jesus was "a friend of tax collectors and sinners" while he was on earth (Matthew 11:19). He is the ultimate example of a friend who "loves at all times" (Proverbs 17:17). And our Friend will never leave us or forsake us (Hebrews 13:5). Jesus is there for us and wants to be *with* us 24/7. Wow.

I hope by now you're beginning to sense that it really is possible to live in such a way that we might one day hear Jesus say "Well done." If we allow Jesus to live through us, of *course* he'll be pleased with us! You and I can do all things through Christ who strengthens us (Philippians 4:13)! Praise his name! Do it *now*!

Our Superior

Of all the ways we can relate to Jesus, there's one that forms the foundation of all others, one crucial distinction that all these facets of relationship have in common. In every aspect of our relationship with Jesus, he is to be our *Lord*. Think about it:

- As our *Savior*, he has earned the right to be our Master. He paid the ultimate cost for us. Paul said, "You are not your own; you were bought at a price. Therefore honor God with your bodies" (1 Corinthians 6:19b-20).
- As our *shepherd*, Jesus directs us and decides where we will go and what we will do. Besides, mere sheep like us aren't smart enough to make those decisions on our own!
- As our *source*, Jesus the vine decides what we need for life, health, and holiness. He is our "all in all," and we are consecrated to bear the fruit he wants us to bear.

- As our *sibling*, Jesus is God's one and only Son, yet he is the "firstborn among many brothers and sisters" (Romans 8:29). In the Hebrew culture of that time, the firstborn son was the superior son with the birthrights. Thus, he was leader over the other siblings.
- As our *friend*, Jesus is ready to help us no matter how much we may fail him. However, he will only call us his friends as we obey him. Jesus told his disciples, "You are my friends if you do what I command" (John 15:14).

I vividly remember an intense conversation I had with the Lord one night during my senior year of high school, while driving in my car. I can even tell you where I was on the road. I was highly upset at God for something he was telling me to do. I didn't want to do it. I didn't see the *need* to do it. And I wanted to know why I *had* to do it. So there I sat, in my car, "having it out" with the King of kings (not something I would necessarily recommend, by the way).

Right in the middle of my ranting, though, God's still, small voice spoke loudly to my heart and got right to the point. He said, "It's none of your business." Needless to say, I wanted some explanation for what I considered to be his rather rude and abrupt comment! God simply and gently reminded me of 1 Corinthians 6:20: "You are not your own; you were bought at a price."

During those volatile years of high school, I needed Jesus to be my shepherd, my source, my sibling, and my friend. But first I had to yield to him as my *superior*. And so must you.

My Daily Response

Of all the ways we can relate to Jesus that we've studied today, which are you most thankful for? In which way do you tend to most often relate to Jesus?

Stop and pray now. Ask the Lord to help you completely yield everything in your life to him. Hold nothing back. If you can, bow before God right now to physically represent your recognition of him as your Lord and Master.

Write out Romans 12:2—by memory, if possible.

JOURNAL

HEAVEN'S
PRAISE

Think once more about the first stanza of "The Servant's Creed." Write it out below. If you need help remembering it, see page 6.

Now put that stanza in your own words. What does your heart long to say to God? Do you truly yearn to know him? If not, be honest with him, and ask him to increase your hunger to know and love him.

For this session, you'll need:

• Nothing. Just *be* there!

START WELL (10 minutes)

Welcome! Let's spend some time getting to know and encourage one another—even if we already *do* know one another. Stand up and get into groups of four.

Allow time for groups to form. If you're meeting for the first time, give group members a few minutes to introduce themselves before moving on.

Now, in your groups, take some time to compliment and congratulate one another for who you are and what you've done. Even if you've never met before today, come up with something nice to say about each person— maybe even give everyone a pat on the back or a hug. Take a few minutes to do that, and then sit together to discuss these questions: → → 1

Give groups five minutes to talk, and then bring everyone back together. Ask for volunteers to share highlights and insights from their discussion time.

We're going to begin our exploration of *Heaven's Praise* as a group. Something you probably already noticed this week as you read on your own is that God often measures success a lot differently than we do. Hopefully though, you've also noticed that we're *already* God's "success stories." But God's not done with us yet. So let's explore together how to live a life that ends with God saying to each of us, "Well done."

RUN WELL (25 minutes)

Discuss together: → → 2

Get back into your small groups. Have a volunteer read Matthew 25:14-30, and then take 10 minutes to discuss these questions: → → 3

→ → **1**
- How did it feel to praise each person in your small group? What was it like being on the giving end? the receiving end? Why?
- When have you received praise—maybe even an award—for something you really didn't have a lot to do with? How did you respond?

→ → **2**
- What's your reaction to the main idea of *Heaven's Praise*—that God actually *wants* to reward and praise each of us? Why?

 MATTHEW 25:14-30

→ → **3**
- What examples of "the Master's" rewards and praise do you see in this passage?

- What roles do the servants play (or not play) in receiving those rewards? What does that tell you about your own role in receiving God's rewards?

- When have you taken the talents God's given *you* and put them on the line for his sake? How has God already rewarded you for your faithfulness?

Bring people back together after 10 minutes. Share highlights and insights from your discussion time.

Let's look at this week's key verse, Romans 12:2. Can someone read that for us? → → 4

FINISH WELL (20 minutes)

Our example for pursuing heaven's praise—and the only one who can make it possible for us to achieve it—is Jesus. So let's look at what heaven's praise looked like for Jesus when he was still on this earth.

Read Matthew 3:13-17, and then discuss these questions: → → 5

Get back into your small groups, and take five minutes to discuss these questions. Then find a partner and set up a date in the coming week to touch base and talk about how you're already hearing God speak and what you'll do in response to what you're hearing. I'll close us in prayer afterward. → → 6

After five minutes, regain everyone's attention. Pray for the group, asking God to open each person's heart to the possibility—and the reality—that God *does* want to praise each of them for a life "well done."

ROMANS 12:2

→ → 4 • Think once more about the idea that God wants to reward and praise each of us. What "pattern of this world" does God need to interrupt in your life so you're able to "test and approve what God's…good, pleasing and perfect will" *is*?

 MATTHEW 3:13-17

→ → 5 • What did Jesus do? What did the Father and Spirit do? What's the connection between their actions?

• Look again at verse 17. How would you be changed if you heard God say this about *you* this clearly?

→ → 6 • How has your perspective about God's rewards been changed or challenged this week? Talk about it.

• How will you respond to that challenge this week?

AIM RIGHT

Locate the Target

DAY 1

Have you ever felt that you've been wandering through life, not quite knowing what exactly God's expecting from you? Sadly, many in God's family spend much of their lives this way. They walk around with an I-hope-so approach to the Christian life—they hope they're doing God's will or hope they're doing what is best and right. Many eventually become discouraged and quit even trying.

Other Christians seem to think the goal of their Christianity is to somehow please God through their endless striving, as though God will love them only when they're performing up to his expectations. But as we learned last week, the Father is already pleased with us, not because of how much good we manage to do, but because we are his children.

Stop now and ask yourself this question: What should the goal of *my* Christian life be, as I live each day? Get an answer in your mind before moving on.

Now look at your answer a little closer. Is your goal measurable? At the end of your day, can you look back and know for sure if or when you hit that goal? Perhaps more important, is the goal you just identified *attainable*? How much control do you really have over whether you can successfully aim at and hit your target?

Let's say, for example, you answered, "My goal is to know God more." That's an incredible answer! After all, "Knowledge of the Holy One is understanding" (Proverbs 9:10b). Paul talked about his deep desire to *know* Jesus—"both the power of his resurrection and participation in his sufferings" (Philippians 3:10). Nonetheless, I do not believe that the best target for us to shoot for each day is "to know God more." Hear me out, and please understand that I agree that knowing God more and more intimately is the *ultimate* goal for each of us in this life. That's why, just last week in fact, I called it "life's greatest pursuit."

However, for a couple of reasons, I believe getting to know God more is *not* the best target to shoot for on a daily basis. First of all, success isn't easily

measured. God is always working behind the scenes in our lives, teaching us his ways and shaping us in the likeness of his Son. Just as kids rarely notice that they're growing taller, we're often not aware of how much, or even *how*, we're growing spiritually day by day.

Furthermore, knowing God better isn't a readily attainable goal. I can't get up on any given day, say to myself, "I'm going to get to know God more today," and then, at the end of the day, be sure I've accomplished what I said I'd do. Certainly I can read the Bible and pray really hard, asking God to reveal himself to me—and I should. But how God helps me know him better, and when he does, is his call, not mine.

Thinking I can decide how deeply I get to know God is like thinking I can decide how intimately I get to know another person. No matter how much I may want to know that person, the degree to which I'll ever actually know him or her depends on what the other person is willing to reveal to me.

It's like that with God, too. In Paul's doxology in Romans 11:33, he wrote, "Oh, the depth of the riches of the wisdom and knowledge of God! How unsearchable his judgments, and his paths beyond tracing out!" Ultimately, only God can help us know God more.

I once heard the story of a grandfather and his grandson fishing on a huge lake. The grandson gazed across the expanse of the lake and said, "Granddaddy, that sure is a lot of water." The wise elderly man looked at his grandson and replied, "Yes, son, it is…and that's only the surface." While God certainly wants to reveal himself to us—and *will,* as we seek him with pure hearts—his will, like the depths of the ocean, will always be "beyond tracing out" on our own. We are utterly dependent on God to make himself known to us.

Love and Obedience

So if knowing God better isn't our best target, what is? What *can* we aim at and hit every day? Or put another way, what does God expect of us, and what is our primary responsibility before him?

Please turn to Mark 12:28-34. What two commandments did Jesus say are the most important? Why do you believe he chose these two?

When we truly love God with everything we are and have, we'll *want* to keep the other commands regarding our relationship with him. We won't value anything more than we value God because all our affection and desire will be focused on him. And when we love our neighbors with a godly love, as Jesus says we should, we won't seek to defraud them or harm them in any way.

Please read what Jesus told his disciples in John 15:9-14. According to this Scripture, what should our love for God lead us to do?

It's not enough to say we love God. We must demonstrate that love by doing what God tells us to do. It's in the doing that far too many professing Christians fall short. Moses told the children of Israel in very straightforward language what their responsibilities were: "And now, Israel, what does the Lord your God require of you? He requires only that you fear the Lord your God, and live in a way that pleases him, and love him and serve him with all your heart and soul" (Deuteronomy 10:12, NEW LIVING TRANSLATION).

True Worship

The word that sums up wholehearted love and devotion to God is *worship*. True biblical worship is adoring God with every part of our being. It's surrendering our lives and all our moments to his will and direction.

The other day I read again about how Abram (which means "exalted father") became Abraham the "father of many."[1] Each time I've read about Abram's calling in Genesis 12, I've been both challenged and convicted by his quick and unquestioning obedience. Listen to how Abram responded to God's directive: "The Lord had said to Abram, 'Go from your country, your people and your father's household to the land I will show you'...So Abram went, as the Lord had told him" (Genesis 12:1, 4a).

Not until this most recent reading, however, did I notice another equally powerful, profound, and revealing fact about Abraham's character. Each time Abraham moved to a new location, the first thing he did was build an altar of worship to God. That tells me that Abraham's walk with God matched his talk. He wasn't obeying God out of fear or for personal gain. He clearly loved and adored the Lord, and he honored God by worshipping him everywhere he went in Canaan. In other words, his love for God *motivated* his obedience.

Have you ever wondered why God's first big written revelation to the children of Israel was a set of ten commandments on two cold, stone tablets? Doesn't that strike you as a bit odd? I mean, wouldn't it have been better for God to have provided a few paragraphs about himself and who he is—you know, have a little "get to know me" time? Why would he choose to unveil all these "thou shalt nots," rather than a few more "I ams"? I believe it's because knowledge of the Holy One requires the right preparation. Before God can allow us to know him intimately, we must love and obey him consistently.

As you go through this second week of our study, my prayer is that you'll discover how to "aim right" at the *best* target of true worship and obedience. By doing so, you'll experience the awesome presence and personality of our precious and powerful God like never before.

Mark Hall wrote a song that became the title cut of Casting Crowns' second album. It's called "Lifesong." Listen to these words from the chorus: "I want to sign Your name to the end of this day, knowing that my heart was true. Let my lifesong sing to You."[2]

Think back over your day today (or yesterday). Did you hit the mark of loving God with your whole being as best you could? Or did you give him only halfhearted devotion and worship? Answer honestly, and ask God to reveal your heart and motives. Write a prayer below that expresses your desire to obey whatever the Lord leads you to do the rest of this day.

{ JOURNAL

WEEK 2 | DAY 1

Read Galatians 2:20 several times, and meditate on the verse. Notice how Paul's words relate so well to aiming at our target of surrender and obedience. Then think about what those words mean to you right now.

Write the first two stanzas from "The Servant's Creed" on page 6. Say them out loud as you write, and let those words be your prayer.

JOURNAL

---

[1] Charles R. Swindoll, ed., "The Beginning of a Nation," *The Living Insights Study Bible* (Grand Rapids, MI: Zondervan, 1996), 20.

[2] Casting Crowns, "Lifesong," © 2005 Club Zoo Music (BMI)/ SWECS Music (BMI) (admin. by EMI CMG Publishing).

HEAVEN'S
PRAISE

Last week we learned the importance of knowing God. "The fear of the Lord is the beginning of wisdom, and knowledge of the Holy One is understanding" (Proverbs 9:10). We must get our thinking straight about who God is and what our relationship with him should be before we can aim straight. So let's review.

Read Matthew 25:14-30. What hints or clues do you find that each of the servants knew and understood who his master was?

Two of the servants knew their master well enough to know what he wanted them to do with what he had entrusted to them. However, even though it was vitally important, *knowing* was not enough. The principle of knowledge should naturally lead us to the second principle in our strategy for success at life: the principle of *intent*.

When the master brought his property to the servants, their first thought ought to have been, "What should I *intend* to do now for my master?" Another way to say it is, "What should I now *aim* to do, now that I know what God desires?" The more we know God—the more we *think right*—the more intense our desire will become to *aim right* at loving him and consistently doing his will.

Aiming the Dart

I did some research online and found instructions for aiming a dart. Here they are: 1) Find a sightline. 2) Lead with your elbow. 3) Know your dominant eye. 4) Aim directly at your target.[3] Sounds simple enough, right? In fact, these simple steps coincide perfectly with what we need to do to aim spiritually. Let's see how, starting today with step 1.

As we prepare to throw a dart, we first need to find a sightline. To do that we need a fixed point of reference at our end of the line. Whether it's a knuckle on the throwing hand or the tip of the dart, we need a fixed point so we can consistently and properly line up our shots. Fortunately, God has provided a wonderful sightline reference point to help us "line up our shots." It's called the Bible.

In Psalm 119:105, David wrote, "Your word is a lamp for my feet, a light on my path." Notice that David talks about two kinds of light here. Let's start with the latter one.

The Hebrew word for *light* in this verse means "illumination" or "luminary." It was used to describe lightning, the sun, or a bright, clear morning. When I think of "a light on my path," I think of driving my car. I prefer to drive in the daytime because I love to see far down the road. If I'm driving at night, I feel more secure with the high beams on. Likewise, it's comforting that God's Word *illuminates* our path, isn't it? It's great when we can see "down the road" of our lives. For example, maybe God has already shown you where you're going to school, who you're going to marry, or when you'll be able to retire. Occasionally God chooses to reveal such things to us. It's always wonderful when God "turns on the high beams" and gives us a look into our future.

But let's face it, often we don't have the luxury of seeing months or years down the road. Sometimes life is so confusing and challenging that we're not even sure what we need to do *next*. Have you ever driven through a dense fog? High beams don't help in the thick mist, do they? In fact, they magnify the fog and make it even more difficult to see. What we have to do on foggy nights is click the lights down to the low beams, so we have only enough light to see a few feet in front of us.

That's why I so appreciate the *other* part of Psalm 119:105. God's Word is "a lamp for my feet." The Hebrew word for *lamp* in this verse refers to light from a candle—a small light focused on one's feet where the light is needed most.[4] God knows when we need the Bible to be our "high beams" to show us what lies ahead. However, God also leads us and shows us what we need to know *today*. If we earnestly and humbly seek God's direction, he'll reveal our next steps when we need to take them. God's Word always points us in the right direction, and it's our perfect sightline!

We can trust the Bible as the authority to lead us. Jesus said to his Father, "Your word is truth" (John 17:17). As Chuck Swindoll puts it, "This is not human counsel within the pages of this Book; it is truth—it is divine counsel…truth you can rely on, truth that will never shrivel up or turn sour, truth that will never backfire or mislead."[5] The Bible has a consistency and flow that baffles the intellectual mind and points us toward the only explanation possible: The Bible is indeed God's written revelation to mankind, both inspired and protected by him.

Grasping the Book

I can't remember who first showed me the hand-and-fingers memory tool when I was a kid, but it has stuck with me for many years now. It shows us five methods to use if we are to firmly "grasp" the Bible for ourselves:

Pinky: Read the Bible. A wonderfully effective way to understand the major themes and characters within each book of the Bible is simply to read it, much as you would read a great novel. I suggest using a daily reading plan, such as the *God Sightings: One-Year Companion Guide* by Group Publishing.

Ring finger: Meditate on the Bible. Psalm 1:1-2 says, "Blessed is the one… whose delight is in the law of the Lord, and who meditates on his law day and night." Reading a passage through once is just the beginning; it's important to read certain verses or paragraphs over and over until you begin to grasp what God's saying to you though them. Listening to the Bible being read or taught is also a great way to meditate.

Center finger: Internalize the Bible. "I have hidden your word in my heart that I might not sin against you" (Psalm 119:11). Hiding Bible passages in your heart is much more than mere short-term memorization—it's internalizing those truths and making them your own. You accomplish this by repeated meditation and deliberate memorization.

Forefinger: Study the Bible. There are deep hidden truths that we'll never unlock unless we dig for them. Book studies, character or personality studies, and word studies are all great ways to discover powerful insights into God's Word. A good study Bible with a concordance and commentary section is also helpful.

Now, before we get to what the thumb represents, try an experiment. Try to lift and hold your Bible *without* using your thumb, using just the other four fingers. Now, with your other hand, try to pull your Bible out of the first hand's grasp.

Then grasp your Bible again in the same hand, but this time use all five fingers, *including* your thumb. Try to pull it out of your hand again. Not as easy, is it?

So what's *our* thumb here?

Thumb: Live the Bible. No matter how much biblical knowledge you or I have, regardless of how many verses and commandments we can quote, we can't grasp the meaning of the Bible if we aren't applying and obeying what we know. We will never firmly grip God's Word until we do what James 1:22 tells us: "Do not merely listen to the word, and so deceive yourselves. Do what it says."

Loving the Book

Read 2 Timothy 3:12-17. What reasons did Paul give Timothy to hold firmly to the Bible?

Scripture held the truths necessary for Timothy to accomplish his mission so that, at the end of his life, he could hear Jesus say, "Well done." Paul wanted God's written Word to be *precious* to Timothy—just as it was precious to Paul.

A few years ago a music group from Russia came to our area and played a concert, which my wife and I attended. The lead singer told a story that to this day makes me shiver. One day, all the children of an elementary school in the Soviet Union were called together by the KGB and made to sit down in their large assembly room. Then one of the KGB sergeants pulled out a Bible and threw it onto the floor in the middle of the room. He cocked his huge machine gun, pointed it directly toward the Bible, and then told the children to line up, walk by the Bible, and spit on it. If they refused, they would be killed. For several minutes, one child after another came within a few feet of that little Bible and, without much thought or hesitation, added their offering to the growing mass of spittle.

Then something extraordinary happened. One little girl chose not to spit on the Bible. Instead, she leaned over and picked it up, ever so carefully. She used her arm to wipe away all the spit. Then she pulled the Bible to her lips and kissed it. At that precise moment, the sergeant pulled the trigger and shot that little girl through the head.

Is God's Word that valuable to *us*?

My Daily Response

Stop and ask yourself how precious God's Word is to you—really. Do you value it enough to be willing to die to honor it? Or would you avoid some harassment or maltreatment by turning away from it? One thing is certain—if you do not love it in life, you won't defend it to the death. Stop now and thank God for his Word. Ask God to help you hunger and thirst to know it—and him—more deeply.

JOURNAL

My Daily Meditation

Since Jesus is the Word made flesh, we ultimately need to make Jesus our aim. Take some time now, to journal some characteristics of Jesus you'd like to see more of in your life. Then ask him to mold you in those areas. If you're physically able, kneel before God as you pray and write, signifying your submission and worship of him.

JOURNAL

---

[3] "Dart Techniques," http://nicedarts.com/aiming_your_darts.html.

[4] James Strong, *Strong's Exhaustive Concordance of the Bible with Hebrew Chaldee and Greek Dictionaries* (Nashville: Thomas Nelson), 216, 5216.

[5] Swindoll, *The Living Insights Study Bible*, 1313.

HEAVEN'S
PRAISE

We learned yesterday that to properly aim a dart, we must start with a sightline. Today, let's look at the second important step: *Lead with the elbow.* Why is the elbow so important?

It's not enough to simply peer down the sightline toward the target. We can line up our shot perfectly, but if the elbow isn't in the correct position as we launch the dart toward the board, it can lead the hand and arm off course—which, in turn, can cause us to miss the target completely.

We need to "lead with the elbow" in our spiritual lives, too. Nothing is more rewarding than starting the day by setting our sights on loving God and then finding, as we look back at day's end, that by his grace we hit our target! Yet all too often we find ourselves feeling totally off track and utterly defeated after only a few short hours. We need to ask ourselves what it is that actually "leads" aim throughout the day. What either moves us *toward* the target of biblical worship or away from it?

Read James 1:22-24. Why do you think James used the analogy of the mirror? *Why* is hearing God's Word and not obeying it like gazing at our reflections and then forgetting what we've seen as soon as we walk away?

The truths we glean from the Bible can fade within minutes as we're quickly distracted by other things that compete for our attention. One of the key words in the passage we just read is *forget.* *What* forgets? Our minds. James was referring to our *thoughts.* He wasn't implying that we should sit and stare at the Bible all day long. Our eyes and our body must focus on other things as we move through our daily activities. But our thoughts should continue to *lead* us toward loving and obeying our Master.

Now read James 1:25. As you read, notice what one needs to do to be blessed by God.

We must continue to look intently into God's perfect law and then *do* it. James understood a powerful and profound principle: Our minds control our bodies, not the other way around. There can be no deliberate action unless it's first prompted by a conscious thought. Our thoughts are the vehicles that transport God's Word off the static pages of our Bible into the reality of our lives. Unfortunately, the thoughts we entertain can also move us *away* from God and his Word.

God's Take

Do you know why God destroyed the earth with a flood? For many years, I assumed it was because the earth's inhabitants acted in ways more evil than anyone could even imagine. Then I looked closer at what the Bible actually has to say about those folks. In Matthew 24, Jesus compared the flood to the judgment to come. But his description of the people in verse 38 as eating and drinking, marrying and giving in marriage makes them sound very normal. They were performing everyday activities.

The other insight we have is found in Genesis 6:5-6: "The Lord saw how great the wickedness of the human race had become on the earth, and that every inclination of the thoughts of the human heart was only evil all the time." Did you catch what that passage gave as the reason? It listed no specific actions or activities. All we know for sure is that their every thought dwelled on *evil*. And it pained God's heart to see it.

Proverbs 15:26 says, "The Lord detests evil plans, but he delights in pure words." (New Living Translation). What God expects to see in us are pure and pleasing thoughts. And no matter how hard we may try, we can't hide our thoughts from him, for "the Lord knows all human plans" (Psalm 94:11a).

How-to Steps

The following steps are not for the faint of heart. However, if you sincerely want to hit the target of loving your Lord every day in every way, taking these steps to discipline your thoughts is vital.

1. Police your thoughts. Can you imagine a community without policemen? In the absence of those who insist that we honor each other and obey the laws, our society would quickly erode into anarchy. When people are left to themselves with no accountability and discipline, they don't get better—they become increasingly more self-centered and destructive.

We wouldn't dream of leaving our communities and streets open to any criminal who happens to come along. That would be dangerous. Yet why is it that we often leave our minds open to all kinds of impure and harmful thoughts? When left to themselves, our thoughts don't naturally improve and flourish with wholesomeness. Rather, they begin to run wild and wreak havoc.

Paul recognized that danger, and he was careful to police his thoughts. Read 2 Corinthians 10:3-6. What words and word pictures does Paul use that make you think of the police or the military?

2. Evaluate your thoughts. Make sure obedience to God always comes first. In 2 Corinthians 10:5, Paul said, "We take captive *every* thought"(italics added). Paul wasn't content just sitting by the roadside watching the traffic of his thoughts go by, so to speak. He wanted to know and inspect every thought that passed through his mind, and that meant being on duty around the clock. Paul didn't take evenings or weekends off. The Bible says that Satan prowls around like a roaring lion looking for someone to devour (1 Peter 5:8). Walking aimlessly and thoughtlessly through our days, watching mindless TV, or carelessly surfing the Internet—these are all potential opportunities for the enemy to sneak up on us. We must be on our guard constantly!

👑 Read Philippians 4:4-9. Rather than being anxious and worried, what should we think about? What should we *do*?

In these verses, Paul lists criteria we can use to inspect our thoughts. You might think of his words as a checklist to use each time you "pull over" one of your thoughts.

👑 Give it a try right now. Randomly isolate and "stop" one of the thoughts running through your head at this moment. See if it "passes inspection," according to Philippians 4:8. Consider each of these criteria carefully, and place a mental or physical checkmark beside the ones you can say yes to. Is your thought a true thought? Is it noble? Is it right? It is pure? Is it lovely? Is it admirable? Is it excellent? Is it worthy of praise?

If you answered yes to these questions, allow that thought to continue on its way. However, if that thought you're inspecting doesn't meet God's requirements, take the next step.

👑 3. *Seize your thoughts.* Read 2 Corinthians 10:5 again. What did Paul do with every thought?

The New King James Bible says Paul brought "every thought into captivity." The word for "captivity" comes from a root word meaning *a prisoner of war.*[6] When a thought doesn't comply with the truths and directives of God's Word, we are to imprison it and no longer allow it to run rampant within our minds.

Once we take a thought captive, we need to put it on trial. Some thoughts are clearly evil, such as lustful or prideful thoughts. Those should be banished from your mind immediately. Other thoughts might simply need some correction or "discipline," so to speak. For those thoughts, there is one more step we need to take.

4. *Subdue your thoughts.* "We are taking prisoners of every thought, *every emotion*, and subduing them into obedience to our Liberator" (2 Corinthians 10:5, THE VOICE). Like prisoners, all thoughts should be subdued into obedience. But whether that means locking them away for life or simply keeping them long enough to properly correct them depends on the individual thoughts.

For example, imagine this thought flashed into your mind: "You're no good, and you don't deserve anything." Now, that statement is not completely true, of course. But it's also not completely false. What we need to do is *correct* that thought. We need to subdue it and adjust it to be sure it represents what *God* says about us. The corrected thought would be: "It's true that on my own I'm no good and that I don't deserve anything but hell. But through Jesus, I am righteous and worthy!"

God's Part

Paul wrote, "The weapons we fight with are not the weapons of the world. On the contrary, they have divine power to demolish strongholds" (2 Corinthians 10:4). Far too many people don't recognize or realize the spiritual aspects of controlling our thought lives. Without God's help—without his *divine* power intervening—you and I will *never* get control over our thoughts. But the good news is, God not only needs to be involved in our thought life, but also *wants* to be! He's only waiting for the opportunity.

My Daily Response

The psalmist prayed, "Search me, O God, and know my heart; test me and know my anxious thoughts" (Psalm 139:23). The standard for every one of our thoughts must be Jesus. Ask God to search your heart now. Do your thoughts properly represent and honor God, or do they tend to dishonor him and lead you away from your target of loving and obeying him? Make time to journal what he shows you now.

JOURNAL

My Daily Meditation

Write out Galatians 2:20. Discipline yourself to meditate on this verse throughout your day today. Make it your personal goal and assignment to carefully inspect and guard your thoughts. Trust God to alert you to any thoughts you need to seize or shun.

JOURNAL

---

[6] James Strong, *Strong's Concordance Greek Dictionary of the New Testament* (Nashville: Thomas Nelson), 164.

HEAVEN'S
PRAISE

The third step in successfully aiming a dart is *knowing your dominant eye*. The dominant eye is the one we rely on most for precise information about positioning. In other words, it is our dominant eye that shows us more exactly the orientation of the target relative to where we are.

To see which eye is dominant, try this: Extend your arm in front of you. Keeping both eyes open, line up your thumb with a distant object. Now alternate closing each eye. Whichever eye is looking directly at the object is your dominant eye.

If you were like me, the eye that was not dominant was far off the mark! No wonder it's so important that we know and only use our dominant eye when throwing darts. As Christians, we have a "dominant eye" to accurately direct us toward our target of loving and obeying God. It's called our *divine nature*.

Read 1 Corinthians 2:10-16. What does Paul say in verse 12 is the result of Christians having the Spirit of God?

Paul makes it clear that a "spiritual man" is one who has the Holy Spirit. He wanted Christians to see that spiritual wisdom is available to us because we have a divine nature within us (Romans 8:11). God's Spirit dwells in our spirit. Therefore, we are equipped to *understand* the deep things of God and what he has prepared for us.

Now read Ephesians 1:17-19. What three things did Paul pray we would "know"? What needed to happen in order for us to understand these things? Paul knew there was no way followers of Christ would ever comprehend the awesome treasures we have available in God unless we could see them through the eyes of our spirit.

The Three Parts of a Person

It's hard to imagine how important our human spirit really is in our Christian lives. Our spirit is *home* to our divine nature! In order to appreciate its role, we need to first recognize that our spirit is but one of three distinct parts. As a human made in God's image, every person is a triune being. We have a spirit, a soul, and a body. No other creature on earth has all of these parts. Paul acknowledged this three-part nature when he prayed, "May your whole spirit, soul and body be kept blameless at the coming of our Lord Jesus Christ" (1 Thessalonians 5:23).

Why is this important to know? Because God, the Holy Spirit, takes up residence in our *spirit*. He does not dwell in our body, which is flesh. He does not live in our soul. Romans 8:16 says, "The Spirit himself testifies with our spirit that we are God's children." Therefore, we live as spiritual men and women when we allow his Spirit to control our spirit, which in turn *directs* our soul and body. Just the opposite happens when we live "according to the flesh" (2 Corinthians 10:2, King James Version). "Fleshly" people allow their bodies, minds, and emotions to lead their *spirits*.

Watchman Nee, in his monumental work *The Spiritual Man*, explains that the human spirit has three main functions. First, it is our *conscience*. No matter how much we may try to justify our actions and motives in our mind, we have a sense down deep inside in our spirit of whether we are right or wrong.

Second, our spirit is our source of *intuition*. Intuition is independent of any outside influence. It comes to us without any help from our minds, emotions, or wills. For example, have you ever sensed or "known" something in your heart although you couldn't quite reason or figure it out in your mind? That may very well have been an example of the Spirit of God speaking to your spirit in his "still small voice" (1 Kings 19:12, kjv).

The third function of the human spirit is *communion* with God. Nee wrote, "Our worship of God and God's communications with us are directly in the spirit. They take place in 'the inner man,' not in the soul or outward man."[7] When we try to worship God with only our minds, we tend to put our idea of God in a box that we can understand and figure out. But that's impossible, since God's judgments are unsearchable and his paths beyond finding out (Romans 11:33)! No doubt that was one reason Jesus told the woman at the well, "God is a Spirit, and they that worship him must worship in spirit and in truth" (John 4:24).

I pray you're beginning to see why it's so vitally necessary to use our dominant eye—the eye of our spirit—as we go through each day. We can't even worship God acceptably unless we worship him in spirit! So we certainly can't hit our target of loving and obeying God if we don't rely on him to teach and direct us.

Trust His Perspective

Read Proverbs 3:5-6. Meditate on this amazing passage by reading it over again and soaking up every word. What part should our own understanding play as we trust and follow God?

The passage in 1 Corinthians you read earlier said, "The Spirit searches all things, even the deep things of God. For who knows a person's thoughts except their own spirit within them? In the same way no one knows the thoughts of God except the Spirit of God" (2:10-11). Isn't it good to know that the Spirit who lives in us and directs us knows everything? He sees the future better than we see the past. Not only does he know what lies ahead for us each day, he even knows *why* we will experience each circumstance, problem, and victory. We can always *trust* the Spirit to show God's will for us—guaranteed! It doesn't matter whether our minds comprehend it. The Spirit doesn't communicate with our minds, but

with our *spirits*. And in our spirits, we know God loves us and will be with us to guide us every step of the way!

We face two realms of reality each day. Our choice of which realm we believe is the *true* reality will determine our actions and the outcome of our days, our weeks, and ultimately our lives. There is, of course, the tangible reality, which is all around us—what we can see with our eyes and hear with our ears. It's the bills lying on our kitchen table and the money (or lack thereof!) in our bank account. It's the pain and sickness we feel in our bodies or the latest news scrolling across the bottom of our TV sets about death, destruction, and uncertain times. These are all real enough, for sure.

But there is another realm of reality, one that is seen only through eyes of faith. And this unseen reality *governs* what is *seen*! The true reality is that God is still in control. God is seated on his throne, watching over us, loving us, and cheering us on!

My Daily Response

At the beginning of our lesson, you did a simple exercise to discover your dominant eye. It's much more important, though, to know your dominant *spiritual* eye.

Think about an upcoming event, or perhaps a situation you're already in, involving your family, your job, or a goal you're working toward. Focus on that event or situation for a few moments. What thoughts come to mind as you look at that situation? Are they primarily thoughts of fear and anxiety? anger and discouragement? Or instead, do you have a sense of peace and calm?

Ask the Lord to show you which eye you normally use to look at your circumstances. If it's not your spiritual eye, ask God to forgive you and restore your faith in his plan and purpose.

JOURNAL

Paul wrote, "Since you have been raised to new life with Christ, set your sights on the realities of heaven, where Christ sits in the place of honor at God's right hand. Think about the things of heaven, not the things of earth." (Colossians 3:1-2, NLT).

If you're near a window or outside, look up at the sky. (And if not, *get* there.) Take time to be in awe of God's creation. Praise God for making all you see. Now try to look beyond the clouds and the heavens. Trust the *true* reality that almighty God is bigger and more awesome than anything you see with your physical eyes. If you know Jesus as Savior, imagine him "coming in clouds with great power and glory" to take you home (Mark 13:26). Raise your hands and voice toward heaven and praise him *out loud* right now for being your Lord and God. Ask Jesus to help you live today in light of his return. Journal what he shows you.

JOURNAL

---

[7] *The Spiritual Man,* Watchman Nee, p.32.

I hope you're feeling at least a little more comfortable by now with the idea that you can hit your target. Think how far you've come in only a few days! You've located the target—which in itself is a huge accomplishment. You've defined it in detail, so you know exactly where to aim. You know how to discipline your thoughts to be sure they move you toward your goal each day.

On top of that, you're aligning yourself with the Bible to make sure your sights are set in the right direction. And you're learning to rely on the Holy Spirit to guide you! That's a call to celebrate, don't you think? I mean, you're practically home free, right? You've got this in the bag.

Well…not quite. It's possible your aim could still be thrown off late in the shot, and you could still miss the mark. "How could that happen?" you might ask. "After all this effort, why wouldn't I hit my target of worshipping and obeying God?"

Perhaps because, down deep inside, you don't really *want* to.

Following Instructions

Throwing a dart accurately requires one more step: *Aim directly at your target.* That sounds easy enough, but apparently there are dart throwers who don't do that. Some people try to aim to the left or right of the real target. The instructions I read online referred to this habit as "lazy darts" and went on to advise me not to overcompensate to make up for a bad throw.

I have to tell you that's where I had a bit of a falling-out with the dart-throwing expert who wrote the instructions. I don't like someone telling me what I can and can't do. What if I want to overcompensate a little? What will it hurt? I do it all the time in golf! I twist and distort my body any way necessary to make up for my slice. It works fairly well most of the time, I might add. So why can't I do the same thing in darts?

Even while I was still fussing and fuming over the expert's instructions, I was suddenly struck with the absurdity of my objections. The guy who wrote that article is an expert. I'm not. That guy's been playing darts and winning games for years, and he can throw circles around me. What do I know compared with what he's learned? Why should I balk at what he tells me to do? I realized at that moment that the only reasonable thing to do was submit—or surrender, if you will—to the wise directions of the master dart player.

There is no one more capable, experienced, and worthy to lead and instruct us than *Master* Jesus. He hit the mark of loving and obeying his Father every day he was on this earth. Jesus never missed. He has earned our complete trust, and he deserves our complete allegiance. And he will settle for nothing less than our full *surrender*.

Achilles' Heels

You may have heard the term *Achilles' heel*. It refers to a vulnerable spot, a fatal weakness. Achilles, the hero of Homer's classic mythological poem, *The Iliad*, was the son of a Thessalian king and an immortal nymph named Thetis. According to one story, Thetis didn't want her son to die, so when Achilles was an infant, she dipped him in the River Styx to make him immortal. Unfortunately, she failed to dip his heel, which she had gripped during the process. As the story goes, Achilles went on to become a mighty and legendary warrior. It seemed nothing or no one could stop him. That proved not to be the case, however. His demise came during the long siege of the city of Troy when a poisoned arrow hit the one vulnerable place on his body—his heel.

Since the story of Achilles is mythical, we can assume that the physical flaw represented a deeper vulnerability. Some believe that Achilles' fatal vulnerability was his pride. Pride kept him from being invincible.

Within each of us lurks a potential Achilles' heel. For some it is lust; for others, pride, greed, or laziness. Every one of us has a weakness in some area— some sort of hidden flaw that threatens to eventually and suddenly topple us. If we don't surrender our secret thoughts and habits to the Lord *now*, they will certainly surface and shipwreck us in the future.

Two Sides to Surrender

Christians often talk about surrendering to God, but how many of us know what surrender really is? What does it mean to yield our lives to him?

There are actually two sides to the biblical concept of surrender, and we need to understand both to fully grasp its meaning. There are the facts about surrender, and then there's the practical application of surrender. Let's start with the facts.

Fact #1: We've already surrendered. In case you're wondering whether you really want to surrender everything to God, let this truth sink in: You made that decision when you said yes to Jesus as your Savior. At that moment, you gave up everything in order to gain Christ. Paul said, "You are not your own; you were bought at a price" (1 Corinthians 6:19b-20a). Jesus told his disciples, "Whoever wants to save their life will lose it, but whoever loses their life for me will find it" (Matthew 16:25).

Fact #2: Surrender means death. Read Romans 6:5-14. As you read, count how many times you see words that refer to death.

Clearly Paul wanted us to understand that we've died with Jesus and that, as a consequence, we are dead to our sin. His brief thesis includes these powerful words: "Do not offer any part of yourself to sin as an instrument of wickedness, but rather offer yourselves to God as those who have been brought from death to life" (verse 13).

The mental picture of biblical surrender really begins to take shape when we understand that we are already dead to ourselves and what we want. A dead man has no rights to life. When we surrender to Jesus, we yield all rights to our lives from that moment on.

Fact #3: Surrender means slavery. If death and loss aren't enough to convince a person to surrender, how about we add one more "benefit" to the lot? If we look a bit further in Romans 6, we see these words: "Just as you used to offer yourselves as slaves to impurity…so now offer yourselves as slaves to righteousness leading to holiness" (verse 19). Everything about a slave's life is dictated to him by his master: where he goes, what he does, who he talks to, what he eats. True biblical surrender means willingly offering ourselves as slaves to Jesus.

As you can see, Paul didn't sugarcoat surrender. It is what it is: giving up everything we have and everything we are and laying it all at the Master's feet. Jesus didn't mince words either. When a rich ruler who kept all the commandments asked what else he needed to do to have eternal life, Jesus gave him a startling answer.

Read that account from Luke 18:18-23 now. Why do you think Jesus made this demand? Why do you think the ruler reacted as he did?

Jesus' demand of the rich young ruler may appear extreme, but in essence, it's exactly what he demands of all of us. Jesus demands that we put no other gods and no other treasures before him.

It's Up to Us, Too

Now, I need to admit something to you. I know I officially "surrendered" years ago when I first trusted Jesus as my Savior. Yet, there are days when I don't really act like someone who's surrendered, and there have been more than a few times you'd have thought I'd brought my old self back to life! In those moments, I didn't live as if I was still *dead* to my sin.

That's why I'm so glad to know there is a "practical" side to my surrender to God. We still live in human bodies. And this fleshly nature of ours hates to give up control. It will keep trying to show its ugly head, *especially* when we're trying so hard to hit our God-honoring target! That's the reason we must choose *each day* to die to ourselves.

Surrendering everything to God may seem hard and unappealing. But once we step through the door of surrender—once we give in and give up our lives, our wills, and our petty "freedoms"—then we walk into the most amazing and warmly lit place, where there's real life and real freedom like we've never known before! It's the joy and freedom of *Jesus* that can come only to those who truly *surrender*!

My Daily Response

Because you've invited Jesus into your heart, he is more than a guest; he is the Lord of your heart. Imagine your heart as a house. Walk through each room now, as you allow Christ to examine its contents. Surrender every room—including every hidden corner and closet—to your Master. Ask him to clean them out and fill them with his light and presence. Journal your response to him.

JOURNAL

HEAVEN'S PRAISE

Reflect on what you learned this week about the four steps that hitting our target requires. In which are you strongest, and which need the most work?

1. Align yourself with God's Word.
2. Discipline your thoughts.
3. Rely on the Spirit.
4. Surrender yourself completely.

Write out Galatians 2:20 again, from memory if possible. Let it be your prayer of surrender. Also write out stanzas 1 and 2 of "The Servant's Creed."

If you're physically able, kneel before your Lord right now. There is nothing that can deal a more powerful death blow to our flesh or more powerfully remind us he is God and we are not. Sing a song of praise or shout to him while you're on your knees.

WEEK 2 | DAY 5

JOURNAL

For this session, you'll need:

- 1 (mostly) round 1- to 2-inch rock for each group of 4 people
- 6-foot strip of masking tape for each group

Leader: Before your session, use your masking tape to make a 6-foot-long line for each group in your meeting area. Put some space between your lines, so groups have room to work. If you're in a small meeting area, combine groups as needed.

EXTRA IMPACT If you have darts and a dartboard available, play a round of darts together. As you play, make a point of talking through each of the elements and applications of aiming right that Dwayne describes in this week's readings.

START WELL (10 minutes)

Point out the masking-tape lines you put on the floor.

Get into groups of four. Each group should then gather at the end of one of the lines. Let's take a minute to do that.

After groups have assembled and lined up, give a rock to the person at the front of each group.

You have one goal—to roll your rock straight down your line and land it as close as possible to the end of the line. You'll each get one try to aim correctly. Once everyone's had a chance, take about five minutes in your groups to discuss these questions: → →1

After five minutes, bring everyone back together, and ask for volunteers to share answers from their discussion time.

We've all missed the mark at one time or another—or more times than we'd like to think about. And as long as we're here on earth, we'll never be perfect. But God *has* given us ways to improve our aim, even in this life. So let's explore how we can hit the mark—especially the marks *God* wants us to hit—more often.

RUN WELL (25 minutes)

Ask for a volunteer to read Mark 12:28-34. Then discuss these questions: → →2

Let's look at this week's key verse. Can someone read Galatians 2:20? → →3

HEAVEN'S PRAISE

→ → **1** • How close did you get to your goal? What would have helped you do better?
- Think about your last answer. Did you put more blame on your circumstances or on yourself? Why?
- How do you usually react when you "miss the mark" elsewhere in your life? Explain.

 MARK 12:28-34

→ → **2** • How does Jesus make our aim simple here?

- In what ways does he make it really, really hard? Be specific.

 GALATIANS 2:20

→ → **3** • How has this verse spoken to you this week? What thoughts or emotions came to mind?

- What's Jesus' role in our "aiming right," according to this verse? What's ours?

- How have you already allowed Jesus to aim you, rather than trying to aim yourself? How has your aim already changed as a result?

Ask for volunteers to read Psalm 119:105 and Ephesians 1:17-19. → → 4

FINISH WELL (20 minutes)

Get back into your small groups. (Pause.)

Let's reflect once more on the four elements of aiming correctly that Dwayne talked about this week, and then take 10 minutes to discuss the questions that follow.

When you're done with your discussion, pray for one another about what you've shared together. Also, make plans to touch base during the week to encourage one another and to talk about what God's doing in your lives.

After your prayer time, you're free to go or quietly hang out until everyone else is finished. May God bless your time together as you seek his aim for your lives! → → 5

1) Find a sightline—rely on God's Word.
2) Lead with your elbow—discipline your thoughts.
3) Know your dominant eye—rely on the Spirit.
4) Aim directly at your target—surrender to God so you go where *he* wants you.

PSALM 119:105; EPHESIANS 1:17-19

→ → **4** • How well can you see where God's aiming you right now? Can you see the road stretch out before you? Are you just trying to see the next step? Or something in between? Describe what you see as best you can.

→ → **5** • How have you already seen ways to improve your aim as you've worked through this week's readings?

• Put aside any false modesty and consider what's the best part of your aim right now. Why?

• Where does your aim need the most improvement? What's one practical step you can take to allow Jesus to coach you in that area?

1) Find a sightline—rely on God's Word.
2) Lead with your elbow—discipline your thoughts.
3) Know your dominant eye—rely on the Spirit.
4) Aim directly at your target—surrender to God so you go where *he* wants you.

ACT RIGHT

DAY 1

Live to Praise

Last week we looked at what it takes to hit a target. But as anyone who's ever made a New Year's resolution can tell you, goals are useless if they're not followed by action! As management guru Peter Drucker said, "Plans are only good intentions, unless they immediately degenerate into hard work."[1]

At some point we have to quit *intending* to do something and actually *do* it. Knowing how to aim a dart matters only if we actually follow through and throw the dart. Would vast knowledge of the game really mean anything if we never played? Would anyone else know or believe we loved darts?

Similar questions apply to our Christian lives. How will people know we love the Lord if they never see us *do* anything that demonstrates our devotion and our adoration of him?

In our anchor parable in Matthew 25, two very important points support the principle of action. First, Jesus didn't commend the servants until *after* they had invested their talents. Secondly, recall what Jesus said to them. He said, "Well done." He didn't say "Well planned," or "Well thought," or "Well intentioned." He didn't commend them for being "well studied." He expected them to *do* something, they *did* it, and then it was *done*—*well* done, to be exact.

I believe every Christian has a specific assignment—certain works we're expected to accomplish on this earth. Paul wrote, "For we are God's handiwork, created in Christ Jesus to do good works, which God prepared in advance for us to do" (Ephesians 2:10).

As I describe the Christian life in terms of doing, I realize that some may misunderstand what I mean. I'm not implying that we can somehow earn our salvation by what we do. Scripture clearly teaches against this: "A person is justified by faith apart from the works of the law" (Romans 3:28). Nonetheless, once we've trusted Jesus as our Savior, we should want to work for him because we are *in* him and devoted *to* him. James put it this way: "Faith by itself, if it is not accompanied by action, is dead...Show me your faith without deeds, and I will show you my faith by what I do" (James 2:17-18).

HEAVEN'S PRAISE

Our Body, God's Temple

Last week we learned that we are made of three parts: spirit, soul, and body. This may sound simplistic, but with which part do we *do* things? Think about it. Consider again our analogy of playing darts. It's the *hand* that picks up the dart and actually throws it. It's not the mind or the eye. They can point the way, but they can't do the deed.

Likewise, our spirits and minds are hugely important in our walk with Christ because from them spring our faith and our motivation to serve him. But we need our *bodies* to accomplish what our minds are thinking and what our hearts desire.

Paul called Christians' bodies "temples of the Holy Spirit" (1 Corinthians 6:19). For that profound reason, Paul said we should "honor God" with our bodies (verse 20). When Paul spoke of a temple, he was no doubt thinking of the Temple in Jerusalem. I want us to look at three parallels we can draw from the Temple that relate to *us* as God's temple now.

First, the Temple was *visible*. In fact, it was impossible to miss! It covered 15 percent of Jerusalem during Paul's day. Just the front porch of the original temple, which Solomon built, stood more than 30 feet high (2 Chronicles 3:4)! It towered above the city. As God's temple, we, too, should be "impossible to miss." Like light in a dark room that cannot be ignored, we are to be light to this world, shining the hope of Christ for all to see.

Second, the Temple was *vibrant*. God's presence dwelt there. Read 2 Chronicles 5. Now read 7:1-3. How did the Israelites respond to God's glory filling the Temple?

Have you ever been around someone who, well, *glows*? You immediately sense something is different about him or her. That person has a passion for God that's contagious. The Spirit seems to "ooze" out whenever you're around that person. We all should be that vibrant—because as followers of Jesus, we all have the Spirit of God inside us.

The third parallel we can draw is that the Temple in Jerusalem was *vital*. It played a major role in Jerusalem and among the surrounding nations. King David said, "The house to be built for the Lord should be of great magnificence and fame and splendor in the sight of all the nations" (1 Chronicles 22:5a). The Temple represented God to the people. It was a place of sacrifice and praise to the true and living God. Laws, customs, and values were all influenced because of the Temple's powerful presence.

Likewise, we are God's ambassadors, his representatives to this world. Jesus said we should be "salt of the earth" (Matthew 5:13). We should "flavor" our communities and our families with the goodness and influence of the Lord.

People who act right are those who behave as if they have the very *life* of God living inside them. For Christians, acting right is more than a mere act—it's participation in an awesome reality! The King of kings and Lord of lords really does live in us and through us! So, since Christ lives in us, we need to ask ourselves, What should a life full of divine vitality look like? With God living inside, how should we *act* on the outside?

Proclaim His Praise

First Peter 2:9 is an amazing verse about how we should act, and we'll be meditating on it throughout this week. Please read it now. What did Peter say we should proclaim? Stop and think of some ways *you* can do that.

Peter calls us a "holy nation" and, in the King James Bible, a "peculiar people." It seems clear Peter is saying our love for God should be obvious to other nations and peoples. And how do we declare God's praise? We praise him with our bodies, which outwardly and *visibly* glorify him.

Imagine you have a child who has really struggled in math. (If you don't have a child, put yourself in the place of the student instead.) You've been concerned about your child's grades because they continue to drop. Then one day your child brings home a score of 100 on a math test! How would you respond when your child showed you the score? You'd probably say something like, "I am so proud of you," or "Great job!" or "I knew you could do it," wouldn't you? At the very least, you'd smile and nod your approval.

Now imagine that, rather than responding like any *normal* parent would, you merely stand there and look blankly at your child. You don't say a word to show your approval. How strange and unnatural would that be? After all, on the *inside* you're filled with excitement and admiration for your child (and thankfulness that he or she might actually *pass!*). Yet, you do nothing to outwardly express your praise.

Let's apply that idea to our Christian lives. How abnormal is it when Christians say they love God yet never willingly and joyfully allow their praise for God to spill out of them? Down inside, they may love God and want to worship him, but they hesitate to express how they feel. For whatever reason, they keep their thankfulness and adoration tucked carefully away. Unfortunately, praise that is harbored inside and never allowed to escape through our bodies isn't really praise at all. And it's certainly not the kind we can "declare" to the nations—or, to bring it closer to home, to our unchurched neighbors and friends.

My Daily Response

This week, you'll be challenged to experience some outward expressions of praise—and perhaps try a few for the first time. One wonderful way to proclaim God's praise is to share your faith story with another person. Psalm 107:1-2 tells us to "Give thanks to the Lord, for he is good; his love endures forever. Let the redeemed of the Lord tell their story." Who might the Lord want you to share his good news with? Who are you praying for and cultivating for the kingdom? Write their names below, and look for opportunities to share with them this week.

JOURNAL

My Daily Meditation

Here's one more parallel to the Temple in the Bible: It was a *visual symbol* of our need for Jesus. The Temple was a place where people offered sacrifices to atone for sin. On the cross, Jesus was the ultimate sacrifice. We, too, should be a place where sacrifices happen, as we turn away from sin and surrender to God's will and his ways.

So the question isn't, What do you want to do today? But rather, What might *God* want to do *through* you? Be still and listen to what God may be saying to you now. Journal a prayer of sacrifice and praise to him.

JOURNAL

[1] Peter Drucker quotes, Thinkexist.com http://thinkexist.com/quotation/plans_are_only_good_intentions_ unless_they/8205.html.

DAY 2 Live to Serve

As a dad, I love it when people say to me, "Your boys act just like you." My kids remind them of me. As God's "kids," we should represent his character and compassion so when others look at us, they'll be reminded of our Father. Jesus said, "A new command I give you: Love one another. As I have loved you, so you must love one another. By this everyone will know that you are my disciples" (John 13:34-35).

We read yesterday in 1 Peter 2:9 that we are to "declare the praises of him who called" us out of darkness into his wonderful light. Our lives should radiate God's praise every day. The best way for us to demonstrate God's excellent ways is to act like him. Therefore, we must serve each other—just as Jesus served us.

Read Mark 10, beginning in verse 35 where James and John make a rather selfish request of Jesus. Read through verse 45, and take note of what Jesus says about serving and being served.

To get a better idea of how serious Jesus is about serving, let's look again at the parable of the talents in Matthew 25. Who gets *commended* in that parable, and who's doing the commending? Is it children who hear "Well done" from their father? Is it siblings who hear "Well done" from their elder brother? Or perhaps, a teacher who passes accolades along to his students? No. Instead, the dominating theme throughout is the master/servant relationship. He uses the words *servant* or *servants* no less than six times.

There are only two inferences in the entire Bible to Christ saying "Well done." And in both passages, the setting is of a master speaking to his *servants* (Matthew 25:14-30, Luke 19:11-27). I think the message is clear. Jesus wants to drive home that only those who faithfully *serve* him will have any chance of hearing him say to them those precious and powerful words, which all Christians should long to hear.

Servants Who Serve

Here's the third stanza of "The Servant's Creed" again:

In serving Christ through serving men,
His praise I will proclaim.

There's something very, very powerful about serving others in Jesus' name. That's because, when we reach out to help someone in need, we're literally serving *Jesus*. As we take food to a shut-in, we're taking food to Jesus. When we help build a home for a low-income family, we're building a home for Jesus. When we

64

take time to encourage someone who's just lost his or her job, we're also encouraging our Lord and Savior Jesus.

👑 Read Matthew 25:34-40. According to verse 40, to whom are we really ministering when we help "the least of these"? Why does Jesus put it this way?

The term *serve* carries two different ideas. The Greek word for servant in Matthew 25 means *slave*.[2] A slave must *serve* his or her master by doing whatever he commands. But when Jesus said in Mark 10:45 that he came to serve rather than be served, the word *serve* doesn't mean as a slave. Instead, the word is best translated "wait upon as a host or friend" or "to minister."[3]

Just as Jesus certainly wasn't enslaved to other people, neither are we. We have one Master and Lord. Jesus wasn't obligated or owned by anyone; he answered only to his Father in heaven. However, he *chose* to serve us—to minister to our greatest need—to be the Savior who would take away our sins. Jesus also set the standard for how to serve others—he willingly "made himself nothing by taking the very nature of a servant, being made in human likeness. And being found in appearance as a man, he humbled himself by becoming obedient to death—even death on a cross!" (Philippians 2:7-8).

A Servant at Heart

The term *servant-leader* has become rather popular. And much of what is written is good and needed. Nonetheless, I'm concerned that some may misunderstand the intent of that phrase. We're not to be servants just so we can lead. That wasn't Jesus' approach at all. It was just the opposite: Jesus was a leader so he could *serve*.

Perhaps a better term would be *leader-servant*, so the emphasis is on *servant*. Or maybe even *servant-servant*—one who's just as content in the background as he or she is up front leading, one whose goal is not to be recognized, noticed, or in charge. If that person needs to step up and lead, he or she is ready and willing to do it. However, if someone else is better suited to lead, that's fine, too. A true servant simply wants the mission to be accomplished and his master to get all the glory.

A great example of a true servant was David Livingstone. Dr. Livingstone was a pioneer medical missionary to Africa in the mid-1800s. One of the most popular national heroes of late nineteenth-century Britain, Dr. Livingstone was widely known for his daring exploits across large portions of southern and central Africa. But it was his passion for lost souls that drove him on. He once said, "I evangelize while I explore. I would give up exploring before I would give up evangelizing." The first printing of the book Livingstone wrote about his adventures was twelve thousand copies. All were purchased within a few hours. But true to form, he used part of his earnings to return to Africa.

Although Dr. Livingstone was famous and somewhat prosperous in his later years, his success came at a great personal cost. He suffered from almost constant fever for ten years, continuing his missionary journeys despite his sickness. He was often separated from his family for months and years at a time. He even endured the death of his wife and a young child while they were with him in the missionary field.

Whenever I hear about someone like David Livingstone, I catch myself asking, "Why would he endure so much and be so determined to serve others, while willingly giving up his own comforts and safety?" I think Dr. Livingstone himself summed it up: "Nowhere have I appeared as anything else but a servant of God, who has simply followed the leading of His hand."[4]

It's one thing to willingly volunteer to be a servant when it's convenient, but what about when God calls us to minister to people we don't know or care for and in places where we're not comfortable, where we don't feel appreciated and welcome? Someone wisely said, "You never know if you have the heart of a servant until somebody *treats* you like one." Where, how, and to whom we minister is *not* something we can pick and choose. Serving as Jesus did is not an "option." Just as our physical hearts beat twenty-four hours of every day, so our spiritual hearts should always be ready to serve—anywhere, anytime, in any way.

When we're ministering to others, and in every aspect of our lives, God is most concerned with our motives. No matter how much we help others and no matter how many cups of cold water we hand out to those in need, if our hearts aren't given to God, and if he is not our Master for whom we ultimately labor, then in his eyes our work amounts to nothing. Jesus said, "Not everyone who says to me, 'Lord, Lord,' will enter the kingdom of heaven, but only the one who does the will of my Father who is in heaven. Many will say to me on that day, 'Lord, Lord, did we not prophesy in your name and in your name drive out demons and perform many miracles?' Then I will tell them plainly, 'I never knew you. Away from me, you evildoers!' " (Matthew 7:21-23).

Once again, we are reminded that doing can never make up for *being*. Jesus must first be our Savior and Lord. And our serving must flow out of our relationship with him.

My Daily Response

Stop right now and take a few moments to praise Jesus for what he did on the cross for you. If you're physically able, bend your knees before him as you praise him. Write a prayer of thanksgiving to your God and Master that he served *you* by dying for you so you could have new life, hope, and peace.

JOURNAL

My Daily Meditation

Only God can shape in each of us a heart to serve—a heart like Christ's. Carefully read John 13:1-17 now, and let Jesus' extraordinary example of a true servant sink into your soul.

Write the first three stanzas of "The Servant's Creed" from page 6.

JOURNAL

---

[2] James Strong, *Strong's Concordance Greek Dictionary of the New Testament* (Nashville: Thomas Nelson), 1401.

[3] Srong, *Strong's Concordance Greek Dictionary of the New Testament,* 1247.

[4] *Inspiring Men of the Faith* (Uhrichsville, OH: Barbour 2008), 172–180.

DAY 3 Live Correctly

The name of today's lesson implies that it's also possible for us to also live *incorrectly*. As reasonable as that may sound, not everyone would agree. Many believe there *is* no absolute standard of behavior, no wrong way of living. Far too many see little need for spiritual beliefs and laws in their lives—they don't want anyone telling them what they can and can't do. For them, truth is relative at best.

In our world today, the line between right and wrong has become so blurred that children often have a difficult time knowing what's acceptable, appropriate, and good. As Chuck Swindoll puts it, "Thanks to the postmodern worldview, it's considered foolish to declare that truth exists and boorish to suggest that one can have it."[5]

I'll admit there are days it would be convenient if there were no absolute truths. Then I could justify my actions simply by saying, "It felt good for me to do that. I liked it. Therefore, it was the right thing for me to do."

I'll never forget the song "You Light Up My Life," which got a lot of airplay back in the late 1970s when I was a teenager. I remember getting upset every time I heard the lyrics in the song's bridge, as the alluring voice of the female artist sang to her lover: "It can't be wrong when it feels so right." I was getting really serious about studying the Bible and trying to do what God wanted. On a few occasions, I literally yelled over the radio with some new lyrics of my own: "It *can* be wrong, even *when* it feels so right!"

Our feelings and opinions will pass away, but God's Word will never pass away (Matthew 24:35). And that *Word* says, "Do not be wise in your own eyes; fear the Lord and shun evil" (Proverbs 3:7). Perhaps the best way to understand and embrace absolute truth is to adjust our perspective of who we are and who we are *not*.

Let's reflect again on our anchor parable, Matthew 25:14-30. Who determined whether each servant's behavior was acceptable and good? More than likely, the servant who hid his talent didn't see himself as lazy. After all, he did *something* with the money—he dug a hole and hid it. His explanation of his action certainly sounds as if he felt justified in his actions.

Now reread Matthew 25:14-30 this way: Take the master out of this story. Pretend he doesn't exist. Without the master to set the standard, without an authority to judge the servant's actions, that servant could go right on believing his own story and holding to his own version of *relative* truth. When's the last time *you* were content with your own version of the truth? Reflect on that for a few moments before reading further.

No matter how much society wants to deny the existence of a Creator, no matter how often we may choose to ignore God's rule over this earth, he is still Lord. No one can take God out of the story. The lord in the parable made it clear that the wicked servant's relative and self-serving idea of truth wasn't truth at all. Likewise, Master Jesus *alone* will determine whether my actions—and yours— are acceptable, good, and right. And *that* is the absolute truth.

What Not to Do

As a small child, I got in trouble with my parents quite often. (Actually, it was more than "quite" often; it was *very* often—like *every day*!) During my times of unruliness, my mom would inevitably say to me, "Dwayne, you had better straighten up and act right!" The truth is, I think she was more interested in what I *shouldn't* do at those moments than in what I should do. Her first priority was for her child to stop acting *wrong*.

I think it's that way with our heavenly Father, too. Before we can live *for* God, we have to turn *away* from sin. From the very beginning of Jesus' public ministry, his message was one of repentance: "From that time on Jesus began to preach, 'Repent, for the kingdom of heaven has come near' " (Matthew 4:17).

God takes our sins very seriously. He knows they hurt us and would ultimately destroy us if not for Jesus. In Jeremiah 5:25, the Lord said to his people, "Your sins have deprived you of good." Our sins are so offensive to God that he will not hear us if we don't turn away from them. Listen to Isaiah's sobering message from God: "Surely the arm of the Lord is not too short to save, nor his ear too dull to hear. But your iniquities have separated you from your God; your sins have hidden his face from you, so that he will not hear" (Isaiah 59:1-2).

In the parable of the talents in Matthew 25, there were three things the servants were clearly *not* to do. These same prohibitions apply to us as Christ-followers today. First, the servants were not to break God's law by stealing their master's money and using it for themselves. God's commandments never change, and they never become outdated.

Second, the servants were not to ignore the wisdom of investing what had been entrusted to them. Although the master didn't specify that they invest the money, two of the three servants figured it out. The Bible is full of wisdom on how we are to invest our lives. And when it's not clear, God will give us all the understanding we need for every situation. But it's our responsibility to ask God for that wisdom and search for it in his Word.

The third thing the servants were absolutely not to do under any circumstance was *dishonor* their master. When my mom would scold me and tell me to act right in front of other people, she was not only trying to protect *me*. She didn't want me to embarrass *her*! My actions were a reflection on her that others would see. While we won't "embarrass" God, we can make him look bad and misrepresent him if we don't obey and follow him carefully.

What We *Are* to Do

What we *should* do, then, is just the opposite of what we shouldn't do. All Christians should 1) keep God's commandments, 2) act wisely, and 3) love and honor the Lord in everything.

Read Micah 6:6-8. What does the Lord require? Where do you most struggle with those requirements right now?

Let's dig into this passage further. To "act justly" is to do what's right and not do what's wrong. Either we keep God's commandments, or we break them. There is no gray area when it comes to justice. God's second requirement, however—to "love mercy"—is not as cut and dried. God clearly wants us to love and embrace his mercy, forgiving people no matter how much they have hurt us. Loving mercy also includes helping the poor and needy. But knowing how much mercy we should show others depends on the particular circumstances. *Wisdom* from God is required to discern each situation.

Therefore, we are to "walk humbly" with God. This is perhaps the most important requirement of all. We must understand that God isn't specifically looking for sacrifice and outward acts of righteousness. What God wants, more than anything, is for us to love and cherish *him*. That should motivate every other act of service we do. Our obedience should flow out of our love and adoration for God.

A good friend heard I was writing on this topic and e-mailed me this note: "A lot of Christians are caught up in trying to lead such clean lives that they are missing out in the *relationship* they have with Jesus. We need a relationship revolution! We fail when our behavior is what we primarily focus on. When we focus first on a real and honest relationship with Christ, then clean living is the outcome."

In my earliest years, I obeyed my parents mostly out of fear of the belt! I didn't want to be corrected the old-fashioned and painful way! But as I grew more mature, I developed a deep respect and appreciation for my parents. My motivation for acting right changed. Sure, I still had a healthy fear of punishment. However, I started wanting to please them simply because I *loved* them. After my dad passed away when I was ten, God knit my heart with my mom's. We grew very close during my teenage years. Any time I even *thought* I might have hurt or disappointed my mom, I would be crushed. In much the same way, I pray I will always honor and love my precious Lord so much that the mere thought of hurting him will detour me from disobeying him.

My Daily Response

Right now, ask God to reveal any hidden motives for the things you do for him. Trust God to forgive you for areas where you may have failed. You may also need to forgive yourself for sins you have committed in the past or attitudes you've been holding on to. Write your prayer to God in the space below.

JOURNAL

My Daily Meditation

Write 1 Peter 2:9 below. What does the verse say God has done for you? Take some time now to thank God for it. Then, journal some specific ways you can declare his praise and be a light to people around you—to your family, friends, co-workers, classmates, and other people you cross paths with today.

JOURNAL

[5] Charles Swindoll, *A Life Well Lived* (Nashville: Thomas Nelson, 2007) 10.

Live Carefully

Let's start again today in the parable of the talents in Matthew 25. What were the servants supposed to do? What did their master expect of them? Or put another way, what was their primary mission? I believe the obvious answer is that they were to *invest* their talents. That was it. We, as God's servants, have the same basic mission: *We are to make the most of what God has entrusted to us.* We are to invest everything God has given us to bring glory and honor to Jesus Christ on this earth.

Stop now. Pray these simple words: "Lord, help me make the most of what you've trusted me with." Then pray it again, this time more slowly and with even more conviction.

As important as that prayer is, how do we pull it off? How do we accomplish our mission of investing what God's entrusted to us? We start by knowing *what* he's entrusted to us. It's hard to invest what we don't even know we have! The servants in Jesus' parable *knew* what their master had assigned to them. Realizing what they *had* helped them know what they needed to *do* in order to fulfill their purpose.

Uniquely You

While the servants in Matthew 25 all had the same general mission, they did *not* have the same gifts. Each was "uniquely gifted," if you will. One was given ten talents, another was trusted with five talents, and the third with one talent.

Let's take some time now to examine how God has distinctly shaped and gifted *you* for his service. As you look closely at these four areas in which God has uniquely shaped each of us, I believe you'll discover some guideposts that can point out God's calling and purpose for your life.

1. *Desires.* Read Psalm 37:3-7. What can we expect to receive if we trust and take delight in God?

According to Strong's Concordance, the Hebrew word for *give* in Psalm 37:4 can also mean to put or make.[6] Thus, I believe we can interpret the idea of God giving us the desires of our heart in two ways—and both are powerfully accurate. God *plants* the desires deep inside those who delight in him, and then he *grants* those desires. What a promise!

I want you to write out some of your hopes and dreams. Yes, right now. Put the deepest longings of your heart before God, on paper. Ask God to guide you as you do this. Because space below is limited, you may need to use the margin or

maybe even a separate notepad, but this is a very important exercise. Take your time. Be thorough.

2. *Resources.* You also need to consider the gifts and other resources God has blessed you with. Read 1 Peter 4:7-11. What have *you* received from God? How can you convey God's grace through those things?
List your God-given resources, particularly those that are unique to you. These should include your talents, abilities, and spiritual gifts, as well as knowledge and experience in particular areas. Resources might be financial or material blessings or relationships you have with others. Again, use as much time and space as you need.

3. *Opportunities.* In *Experiencing God*, Henry Blackaby wrote, "If you keep your life God-centered, you will immediately put your life along side His activity. When you see God at work around you, your heart will leap within you and say, 'Thank you, Father…for letting me be involved where You are.' "[7]
Look around you now. Ask God to bring to mind where he's already working in your family, church, community, and the world. Which of these God-activities could you come alongside in some way? It's OK if you're not sure. Just list what you sense God impressing on you as *possible* opportunities for you.

4. *Peace.* One reliable way to process every decision we make and every direction we take is to note whether we have God's peace in our hearts. Colossians 3:15 begins with these words: "Let the peace of Christ rule in your hearts." The *Good News Translation* puts it this way: "The peace that Christ gives is to guide you in the decisions you make."

The peace of God transcends our human understanding and guards our hearts and minds (Philippians 4:6-7). The dreams the Lord has placed inside you and the mission you feel he's called you to complete may seem impossible. You may feel that your abilities are far from adequate and that there are no clear opportunities around you. But you can't lean on your own logic and understanding. You must trust and settle for *nothing less* than God's deep, abiding peace.

Guideposts and Boundary Lines

Perhaps you noticed that the beginning letters of each area of differences—our *d*esires, *r*esources, *o*pportunities, and *p*eace—spell *drop*. Within each of these areas are directional signs the Lord has *dropped* into our lives. These guideposts point us toward God's plan and purpose for us—if we'll only take time to *look* for them.

Guideposts are the result of what we have from God. But what about what we *don't* have? How might we interpret a *lack* of desire, resources, opportunities, or peace? I believe the fact that God has not given us certain things may at times be *boundaries* for us, alerting us about directions we don't need to take.

God places both permanent and temporary boundaries in our lives. If a boundary is permanent, then thank God for it and accept it. Recognizing and submitting to our immovable boundaries saves us from wasting time and going outside God's plan for us. On the other hand, if you think it might be only a temporary barrier, ask God to remove it or to help you find ways to move through it. Just be sure you wait on God's timing, and don't try to impatiently plow through on your own strength.

A Personal Example

When I was fifteen, I had the opportunity to take a trip which helped solidify God's direction and mission for my life. A pastor asked me to help him lead a series of revival services in New Jersey. I vividly remember flying into Newark Liberty International Airport on my first-ever flight and looking down with wide-eyed wonder at the huge city sprawled beneath us. Even before we touched down, God had already begun burdening my young heart for the families in the houses below. Everywhere I went throughout that amazing week, I sensed a crushing emptiness and void in many of the people of that area.

I'll never forget the burden and resolution in my heart as I flew back home. I was certain God was calling me to share the gospel with people outside the Bible Belt of the South where I grew up. The overwhelming peace the Holy Spirit put in my heart became a *guidepost* for my decisions about how and where I should invest much of my time and resources.

Although God was confirming in my heart a call to national missions, I did *not* sense he was leading me (at that time, anyway) toward *inter*national missions. Now, please don't misunderstand me here. I'm not saying I didn't care for the souls of those overseas. Nor do I mean to imply that I felt completely "off the hook" for them. But God had not placed that burning desire in me or given me that opportunity.

In essence, God gave me a temporary boundary during my early years. He has since removed that boundary and graciously given me freedom to invest my time and resources in helping churches and Christians in several nations around the world.

Let me make something clear: Having an exclusive mission from God in no way means we should never help in other areas or step outside our "special gifting" from time to time. As we studied earlier this week, our first and foremost calling is to be a *servant*—anytime and anywhere.

Nevertheless, God-placed boundaries free us from unnecessary guilt and the false assumption that we must try to fix everything that goes wrong and help everyone who has a need. Even Paul, the greatest missionary ever to live, was not expected to preach to every corner of the world. In fact, the Holy Spirit *prevented* him from going to Asia (Acts 16:6). Yet, Paul knew the Lord Jesus had given him a special mission, and he *completed* that mission (Acts 20:24; 2 Timothy 4:7).

I am thankful that, early in my life, God helped me see the incredible value of knowing and living according to the tailor-made plan he has for me. Recognizing and embracing our God-placed guideposts and boundaries not only helps confirm our mission but can also save us precious time and energy and keep us focused on the special purpose for which God *uniquely* created us.

My Daily Response

Read back through what you wrote today. Underline anything that stands out to you as a possible guidepost—something that confirms your unique purpose.

Look at what you underlined, and place a check beside the ones you're developing and actively trying to invest for the Lord. Put an X beside any assets and blessings you have thus far neglected and not tried to invest.

Based on what you've studied and sensed from the Lord today, what do you feel your specific purpose and mission may be? Journal your thoughts.

JOURNAL

As we saw in Psalm 37:4, God grants our desires when we *delight* in him. Think of a hymn or praise chorus you know. Sing it before God right now. Express your delight in knowing him as your Savior and Lord as you praise him. Imagine him smiling at you at this very moment, as *he* takes great delight in *you*.

JOURNAL

[6] James Strong, *Strong's Concordance Hebrew and Chaldee Dictionary* (Nashville: Thomas Nelson), 5414.

[7] Henry T. Blackaby and Claude V. King, *Experiencing God* (Nashville: Broadman & Holman, 1994), 32.

HEAVEN'S PRAISE

As I'm writing these words, we've just reopened our pool for the summer. The water is still a little cold. This morning, my older son wanted me to push him in. He just couldn't find the courage to jump in the first time on his own.

God knows we all need a push sometimes, too. No doubt that's why the statement "Don't be afraid" is found so many times in his Word. In fact, it's the one statement Jesus made more than any other.[8]

It's not enough to *know* what God's directing us to do; we must have the courage to "jump in" and start doing it. Let's face it, the *doing* part can be downright scary and intimidating at times! One of the many awesome things about our God, however, is that he *knows* our fears. God created us with the ability to *be* afraid, so he doesn't belittle us when it happens! But God isn't content to leave us there, either.

Even heroes of the faith experience fear. Often when God revealed his plans to someone in the Bible, the first thing he did was confront that person's feelings of panic and dread. Read the following verses. Underline the reason(s) not to fear that each person or group was given.

- "David also said to Solomon his son, 'Be strong and courageous, and do the work. Do not be afraid or discouraged, for the Lord God, my God, is with you' " (1 Chronicles 28:20).
- "After this, the word of the Lord came to Abram in a vision: 'Do not be afraid, Abram. I am your shield, your very great reward' " (Genesis 15:1).
- "Hear, Israel: Today you are going into battle against your enemies. Do not be fainthearted or afraid; do not panic or be terrified by them. For the Lord your God is the one who goes with you to fight for you against your enemies to give you victory" (Deuteronomy 20:3-4).
- "You will not have to fight this battle. Take up your positions; stand firm and see the deliverance the Lord will give you, Judah and Jerusalem. Do not be afraid; do not be discouraged. Go out to face them tomorrow, and the Lord will be with you" (2 Chronicles 20:17).

What do you see? Which of these reasons resonate most with you right now, as you face the challenges God has called *you* to?

Replacing Fear With Faith

Promises like the ones we just read are powerful. They calm the nerves and strengthen the hearts of people who desperately need reassurance. There's plenty of advice out there for how to overcome fear, but God's is the simplest and surest. God wants to replace our fear with confidence in *him* and in his promises to us.

Jude 1:20 tells us we should build ourselves up in our "most holy faith." But exactly how do we do that? The answer, I believe, is to pay careful attention to what God tells us and shows us.

Let's look closely at two examples where God gave his followers a specific message, which in turn produced—or should have produced—bold faith in them.

First, turn to Acts 27, and read the fascinating story of Paul's experience as a prisoner sailing to Italy. Take special note of what Paul said would happen on the journey. What gave him such confidence about the future?

Now read Luke 8:22-25. Why do you think Jesus asked his disciples, "Where is your faith?" And for that matter, where *was* it?

These two stories are among my favorites in all the Scriptures. I love how God told both Paul and the disciples what would happen to them and then came through just as he said he would. That powerful correlation is fairly obvious to spot in the account of Paul in Acts. Paul told those on the ship that an angel had warned him about the unavoidable shipwreck—and Paul took the angel at his word. However, in the account of the disciples in the storm, it's easy to overlook what the disciples should have heard.

So why did Jesus rebuke his disciples with that question about their lack of faith? After all, they were in the middle of the mother of all storms. And where was Jesus? He was below *asleep,* for crying out loud! I can just imagine what they were thinking: "Jesus got us into this mess! Now he's brought us out here to die! He told us we're going to other side of the lake, but now the guy with all the superpower is sleeping, and we're drowning!"

Wait. Stop right there. Did you catch what those disciples apparently failed to realize? They *knew* what he had told them, but for some reason they didn't take him at his word—they didn't *choose* to believe him. Before they ever left the bank, Jesus said, "Let's go to the other side of the lake." That should have been enough. There was only one place they were going, and that was all the way to the other side. Jesus doesn't mince words. What he says, *goes.* No wonder he could sleep through the storm. Why worry? And no wonder he said to his disciples, perhaps with disappointment in his voice, "Where is your faith?"

Risk Management

I suspected for years that my tolerance for risk was low. Then I took a quiz online, and confirmed my suspicions. It turns out that, when it comes to investing my money, I have very little faith and courage.

For example, here's one of the questions: Imagine there's been a decline in the stock market, but your own stock hasn't been affected. Now, a month later, the value of your stock is up 50 percent, and you have no information on why this is happening. So what do you do? 1) Buy more, 2) Sit tight and hold on to your original position, or 3) Sell it, put the money into your savings account, and call it a day.[9]

I don't know about you, but I quickly opted for number 3! The last thing I would want to do in a market decline is buy more! I'm way too much of a scaredy-cat for that!

When it comes to taking risks, I can relate to how Max Lucado, in his powerful book *Fearless*, puts it. "Fear," he writes, "feels dreadful. It sucks the life out of the soul, curls us into an embryonic state, and drains us dry of contentment… When fear shapes our lives, safety becomes our god. When safety becomes our god, we worship the risk-free life."[10]

The servants in the parable of the talents didn't have the option of a "risk-free life." Their master expected them to invest what had been entrusted to them. And that required courage—courage to take huge risks. There's a commonly accepted principle in investing known as the risk-return trade-off. According to this principle, the return we can expect from an investment rises with an increase in risk. Invested money can bring higher profits only if there is a possibility that the money could be *lost*. Therefore, to get a 100 percent return on their money, what did the servants in the parable have to be willing to risk? *Everything*.

To fully appreciate what the servants risked, we need to understand how much the master entrusted to them. Several Bible translations, including the King James Bible, refer to "talents," which were worth more than a thousand dollars. The New Living Translation describes what the master entrusted to his servants as bags of silver. In the Contemporary English Version, the servants received five thousand, two thousand, and one thousand coins. In any case, each of the servants received a fortune.

You and I may not have millions of dollars, but what we do have are immeasurably precious gifts and resources, which our Lord has entrusted to us. And we have a mission to invest those resources for God's glory and honor.

Think about the servants once more. Did it really matter whether their risk level was high or low? Did any of them seriously think they could use their lack of faith and courage as an excuse when their master returned? Bottom line: If they were to please their master, did they really have a choice but to risk it all for their master, who expected nothing less from them?

The lazy and wicked servant hid his talent in the ground. Why did he do that? Because he was *afraid*. To live out God's purpose in our lives, we must overcome our fear and live courageously for him, no matter the risk.

My Daily Response

What is your risk-tolerance level when it comes to what God's called you to do? Are you willing to risk failure and regret? discomfort and change? rejection and ridicule?

Take some time right now to be honest before God. Admit your fears and anxieties. Commit to diving into his Word and praying faithfully for his direction. Take courage now as you hear your loving Lord whisper to you, "I am with you." Journal your thoughts and your prayer.

JOURNAL

Write out 1 Peter 2:9. Also, write the third stanza of "The Servant's Creed" on page 6, by memory if possible.

Before we can publicly praise our Lord the way he deserves, we need to praise him in private. Psalm 63:3-4 says, "Because your love is better than life, my lips will glorify you. I will praise you as long as I live, and in your name I will lift up my hands."

Speak out now. Tell God why you love him and why he is so awesome to you. As you're praising God with your lips, lift up your hands to him, both in surrender and in desperate need of his majesty and mercy. Don't rush. Praise God passionately, because he is worthy!

---

[8] Max Lucado, *Fearless* (Nashville: Thomas Nelson, 2009), 11.
[9] "Do you like investment risks? Dare you to find out," Bankrate.com, http://www.bankrate.com/brm/news/investing/20011127a.asp.
[10] Max Lucado, *Fearless*, 10.

For this session, you'll need:

- Dark meeting place. Have enough light for group members to find their seats as they come in, but no more than that. Also make sure you can make your meeting area totally dark later on—cover windows or shut doors to other rooms, as needed.

- Whiteboard or blackboard

START WELL (15 minutes)

Welcome everyone to your darkened meeting area. Once group members are settled in, turn off the lights completely. (Make sure you read the next paragraph, so you can at least paraphrase it once the lights are out!)

I want each of you to do something everyone would see if the lights *were* on. Gesture with your hands, stand up and do a dance—whatever you want. The only rule is that you can't make any noise. Let's take 15 seconds to "do our thing," and then we'll talk.

After 15 seconds, turn the lights on. It's OK if people are still moving—it will add to the fun if they're "caught." Then discuss: → → **1**

Ask for volunteers to read Matthew 5:14-16 and 6:1-4. Then discuss: → → **2**

This week, we've moved from thinking and aiming right to actually acting right. It's great to know the right things, but there comes a time we need to do them. And this week is when we look at how to start making things real in our own lives. Let's explore together how we can make that outward shift.

RUN WELL (20 minutes)

Have people get into groups of four, and then regain their attention.

I'd like to quote something from this week's reading. Think about it as I read: "[O]ur spirits and minds are hugely important in our walk with Christ because from them spring our faith and our motivation to serve him. But we need our *bodies* to accomplish what our minds are thinking and what our hearts desire."

→ → **1**
- What were you doing while the lights were off?
- Could you figure out what anyone else was doing? If so, how did you figure it out?

 MATTHEW 5:14-16; 6:1-4

→ → **2**
- How do you bring these two seemingly contradictory statements from Jesus—from the same sermon—together? How would our activity in the dark help explain it?

- When has Jesus helped you be a light to others? Be specific.

In your groups, discuss the question below that quote. Then read our key verse, 1 Peter 2:9, and discuss the questions that follow that. Let's come back together in 10 minutes: → → **3**

Gather everyone's attention after 10 minutes, keeping people with their groups. Ask for volunteers to share highlights and insights from their discussion time. Ask for another volunteer to read 1 Peter 4:7-11, and then discuss this question together: → → **4**

Write people's answers on your whiteboard, thanking them for their contributions.

Those are all great ideas! As we've studied this week, it's important not only to think right but to act right, as well. It's also critical that, as we act right, people realize what—or rather, *who*—is really motivating us. So let's take this lesson one step further.

FINISH WELL (20 minutes)

Turn back to your groups. If it's possible, put some extra space between your groups right now. (Pause.)

Think of a song, any song you'd like. Don't say it; just think it. (Pause.) **Everyone got a song in mind?**

Good. Now you're going to share your song with your group. Don't worry; you won't have to sing it. What you'll need to do is clap it—a verse and chorus should be enough to give everyone a chance to guess. Let everyone try to guess your song, and then go on to the next person.

Make sure everyone gets a turn sharing a song. When you're done, take 15 minutes to discuss these questions: → → **5**

Gather everyone's attention after 15 minutes. Encourage group members to touch base during the week to talk about what God's doing and saying in their lives—and what they're doing in response.

Close your group in prayer, asking God to help each person put his or her faith into action—and in such a way that others see that faith in action.

HEAVEN'S
PRAISE

> "[O]ur spirits and minds are hugely important in our walk with Christ because from them spring our faith and our motivation to serve him. But we need our *bodies* to accomplish what our minds are thinking and what our hearts desire."
>
> —Dwayne Moore

→ → **3** • When do you find your spirit and mind headed in one direction and your body headed…well, nowhere? Why do you think that happens?

 1 PETER 2:9

• How easy or difficult is it for you to see yourself the way Peter describes you here? Why?

• How do you think the way you see yourself affects how and when you show God's goodness to others?

 1 PETER 4:7-11

→ → **4** • What are some ways, mentioned in this passage or from your own experience, that we can act out what the Spirit's prompting us to do?

→ → **5** • How well did you do at guessing each other's songs? Who was the best guesser?
• What would have helped you guess better (besides singing)?
• Think about what Jesus is doing in your life right now. When—and why— are you only "clapping" when you should be "singing"? Give examples.
• What's one way you can put your faith and action together, so others can see the connection between them as clearly as you do?

STAY RIGHT

Through the Daily Grind

DAY 1

Knowing we've been given certain missions in life—and knowing what those missions are—should place some healthy stress on us to see them through. Our time here is short. Thus, we should have a sense of urgency that spurs us on and keeps us alert. Jesus said, "We must quickly carry out the tasks assigned us by the one who sent us. The night is coming, and then no one can work" (John 9:4, New Living Translation). Like Jesus, we should be occupied with our Father's business, doing the works he's prepared us to do (Luke 2:49, Ephesians 2:10).

Let's reflect on that statement for a moment. We know what we just read is true and important. But sometimes such lofty spiritual goals can feel a bit overwhelming—like yet one more thing we have to add to our already impossibly long list of things to do. Meanwhile, in our "real" world, crises happen. Deadlines happen. *Life* happens. Bosses breathe down our necks. Kids demand our undivided attention. We have groceries to buy, bills to pay, errands to run, and things that seem to constantly break down and need fixing. It's easy to get caught up in just trying to get through the craziness of our day. But what we end up experiencing is a lot of very unhealthy stress and worry.

On top of everything else already pressing on us, we try to squeeze in doing the "God's mission" part. It's easy to feel like we're adding even more stress. Yet, for us to have the chance to hear God say "well done," we've got to somehow weave our life's purpose into the daily fabric of our lives.

When the master in Matthew 25 commended the two servants who wisely invested his money, he called them "good and faithful." *Faithful* comes from the same root word used to describe Stephen in Acts 6:8. Saying he was "full of faith" (King James Version) meant Stephen was constant in his convictions and his reliance on Jesus.[1] Therefore, for you and me to do "well" by Jesus' standard, we need to do more than merely act right from time to time; we must form a pattern of living according to God's specific plan for us. It's nice to talk about being constant in our convictions, but consistency isn't determined by what we do next week or next year. Faithfulness is about what we do with each little decisive moment *today*.

HEAVEN'S PRAISE

Here's a real-life case in point: I'm under a deadline to finish this lesson and get it to my editor. I've worked all day and now into the evening on it. I don't really "have time" to stop and do a Bible study with my sixth-grade son tonight. I know teaching my children God's Word is a huge part of my responsibility as a father, but I'm busy. Can't I just put it off until a later, more convenient day?

I already know what I should do, by the way. However, the verdict is still out on whether I'll actually follow through on my convictions.

Busyness and Fatigue

Getting too caught up in, and beaten down by, the daily grind of life can lead us away from God's plan. We can easily fall victim to "mission-killers."

The first mission-killer is *busyness*. Our schedules can become so packed that we have little or no time left for God. To combat this busyness, we must learn to say *no* to things that aren't critical to our mission and purpose.

In their book *Boundaries*, Henry Cloud and John Townsend call the word *no* "the most basic boundary-setting word." As they explain, "Sometimes a person is pressuring you to do something; other times the pressure comes from your own sense of what you 'should' do. If you cannot say no to this external or internal pressure, you…are not enjoying the fruit of 'self-control.' "[2]

Not only must we say no to what's not necessary, we must also learn to say yes to what is. Read Luke 10:38-42. Which sister—Martha or Mary—was Jesus most pleased with? More important, *why*?

Mary chose to sit at Jesus' feet and learn. Perhaps if Martha had also taken time to listen to Jesus, she, too, would have known what he wanted her to do. Then, rather than chiding her for overloading herself and feeling frustrated about the load she'd created, Jesus could have instead commended her.

It's important to note that Jesus wasn't putting Martha down for working. Jesus himself said he had work to accomplish while he was on earth. Yet Jesus never advocated being "busy." Although he had an enormous mission to accomplish in only three short years, he never seemed in a hurry or too preoccupied to stop and help someone. He was never too busy to fulfill the mission he was put on earth to do.

Busyness is almost always followed by a second "mission-killer"—fatigue. Galatians 6:9 warns us not to "become weary in doing good, for at the proper time we will reap a harvest if we do not give up." I once heard an evangelist say, "If you're weary in well-doing, you're not doing well." God's not impressed when we constantly push ourselves and wear ourselves out—even if it's in the name of ministry. He created us to need rest, and he wants us to have it. Psalm 127:2 teaches us, "In vain you rise early and stay up late, toiling for food to eat—for he grants sleep to those he loves."

I learned early in life what it means to burn the candle at both ends. As a teenager, I worked at four different churches every week, leading their youth and adult choirs. On top of that, I was president of the Christian club at my school and directing a Christmas play there, all the while trying to keep up my studies! I vividly remember one Sunday afternoon when I was completely exhausted. I literally did not think I could go another step. I was scheduled to do a concert at a church in our area that evening, but I was so tired my mom had to drive me. Needless to say, I wasn't doing "well."

As soon as I got to the church, I found a small, quiet room. There I laid my head back and closed my eyes. All I knew to do at that moment was fall on God's mercy and grace. I asked him to forgive me for allowing myself to get so worn down and to help me get through my concert. As I did, something amazing and miraculous started to happen. God brought to my mind one of my all-time favorite Scriptures, Isaiah 40:30-31. "Even youths grow tired and weary, and young men stumble and fall; but those who hope in the Lord will renew their strength. They will soar on wings like eagles; they will run and not grow weary, they will walk and not be faint." I will never forget the way God literally renewed my physical strength on the spot in those few minutes of silent meditation! I was completely refreshed and energized for my concert.

Looking back on that experience, I so appreciate God's grace to renew me as he did, but I'm even more thankful for what he taught me in the weeks and months that followed. I learned to prioritize the activities and projects I was involved with. I relinquished some of my responsibilities and jobs altogether.

Putting in the Rocks

One of the most helpful lessons I've learned over the years is to look ahead and "put in the rocks," so to speak. You might be familiar with the following illustration: A professor placed large rocks inside a gallon jar and then asked his class "Is it full?" When his students said yes, he placed smaller rocks around the large ones. For a second time, he asked, "Is it full?" Again the students said yes.

The wise professor then poured sand into the jar, filling in the cracks between the rocks. "Is it full?" he asked again. By now the students were getting the idea, so they said no. "You're correct," replied the professor. He then picked up a glass of water and poured it into the jar, filling it even more.

The point is this: Our schedules are going to fill up, one way or another. We'll either invest our time each day, or we'll end up wasting it—or, more likely, we'll do some of both. If we're to live out our purpose, we need to determine what our "rocks" are—those things that advance God's mission for us—and put them in our lives first.

(Speaking of what's important, I did finally give in to the Spirit's promptings. I stopped today's writing and did the Bible study with my son. Now, if I can just live out my priorities *every* day...)

My Daily Response

Make a list of everything you have to do this week. Include every responsibility and activity you might possibly have. Take your time; be as thorough and detailed as you can. You may need to use the margin or a separate notepad to be sure you have enough room.

Feel overwhelmed? You don't need to. Lay your list before the Lord right now. Ask God to give you wisdom to know what *he* wants you to focus on.

Now, look at your list. Write an R beside the rocks—the things you need to prioritize. Place a D beside the activities you can delegate to others who can do the tasks at least 80 percent as well as you could—or better. Cross out any activities that aren't urgent or even important (watching mindless TV, for example).

Our meditation verses for this week are Hebrews 12:1-2. Read the verses through several times, taking note of what the passage teaches us about staying right until our time on earth is complete. Write the passage below.

JOURNAL

Psalm 46:10 says, "Be still, and know that I am God; I will be exalted among the nations, I will be exalted in the earth." Stop now. Be very still and silent. Let God restore your strength and renew your mind in this moment. Then raise your hands in the air, and praise God aloud for his grace and mercy. Thank God in advance for helping you say yes to what's important this week and no to what's not.

[1] James Strong, *Strong's Concordance Greek Dictionary of the New Testament,* (Nashville: Thomas Nelson), 4102.

[2] Henry Cloud and John Townsend, *Boundaries* (Grand Rapids, MI: Zondervan, 1992), 36-37.

HEAVEN'S PRAISE

"How can we be so dead when we've been so well fed? Jesus rose from the grave, but you, you can't even get out of bed!"[3] Keith Green wrote those provocative and convicting lyrics more than thirty years ago, but they might as well have been written last week for me.

I tried for several days to write today's lesson on staying right and faithful to God through the good times of life. And I kept hitting a wall. Then a couple of days ago, the Lord woke me at 3 a.m. to show me why I'd been unable to write this lesson.

It was because *I* wasn't staying right during *my* good times.

Now mind you, I hadn't been immoral or unethical. I hadn't stolen anything or spread vicious gossip. I didn't even drop out of church or stop praying over my meals. In fact, I'd been doing all the outward religious things people are used to seeing me do. Yet God showed me discrepancies in some personal habits, and in matters of my heart which only God can see, between who I claimed to be and who I really was. *I* was the one who wouldn't "even get out of bed" some days to spend time with God. The truth is, I'd allowed myself to become somewhat content—even a bit prideful—with my spiritual "accomplishments" and knowledge, and my feelings of self-satisfaction were draining me of my love for God and others.

How could this happen? How did you not see this coming, Dwayne? The same way you might not see it coming. Comforts and pleasure can insulate us and numb our spiritual senses. They can dull our passion for God. Prolonged ease tends to give us a false sense of security in our possessions, circumstances, government, and other people. If we're not careful, we can become more fond of our "comforts of home" than we are of our commitment to our *final* home, heaven.

For those very reasons, good times may be among the most hazardous to our spiritual health. Listen to what Paul wrote to the church in the affluent city of Corinth: "What I mean, brothers and sisters, is that the time is short…those who use the things of the world [should live] as if not engrossed in them. For this world in its present form is passing away" (1 Corinthians 7:29, 31).

As the children of Israel prepared to go into the Promised Land, Moses knew the danger of becoming too engrossed in the things of the world. Read Deuteronomy 6:10-12. What warning did Moses give Israel in verse 12? How would Moses phrase that to you today?

Please note that neither Paul nor Moses was implying that riches are bad. Financial and material prosperity is a blessing from God. The question, then, is not whether we have possessions, but whether possessions have *us*. First Timothy 6:17 says, "Command those who are rich in this present world not to be arrogant nor to put their hope in wealth, which is so uncertain, but to put their hope in God, who richly provides us with everything for our enjoyment."

One of my heroes in the faith is David Green, founder and CEO of Hobby Lobby, a chain of more than four hundred stores that gross well over a billion dollars in sales each year. I've had the privilege of knowing David and working with him over the years. From his humble and unassuming demeanor, you'd never know he was a billionaire. What I admire most is how he's careful to invest what God's blessed him with. In fact, in his book, *More Than a Hobby,* he says one of his life goals "is to use my resources to present Christ to as many people as I can."[4]

Faithful Abraham

Like David Green, Abraham was a man who had great wealth, yet his heart and hope were set above. He was never influenced or controlled by his possessions and comforts. Perhaps that's why God could trust him with so many. Let's look at two examples in Abraham's life that demonstrate his commitment to God, despite his earthly goods.

Read Genesis 12:1-5. As you read, notice what age Abram was when he was called to uproot his home and family. Try to imagine how difficult that must have been to do.

Although Abram had lived in Haran for many years, he willingly moved his family and "all their possessions they had accumulated" (verse 5). And he no doubt had a ton of possessions to move. According to Genesis 13:2, Abram was "very rich in livestock and in silver and gold." Nonetheless, Abram chose to follow God rather than do what was convenient and comfortable.

Now let's fast-forward some forty-plus years. Abram's now Abraham, and he finally has a son to be his heir. God can fulfill the great covenant he made with Abraham to make him the father of a great nation. Talk about things going your way! Life is good for Abraham. All his dreams are coming true. And more than all his riches combined, his greatest earthly possession by far is his precious son, Isaac. Yet, right in the midst of Abraham's "best of times," he's forced to make the hardest of choices.

Read Genesis 22:1-14. What does Abraham's choice to obey God say about his passion and desire to please him?

There's only one way we can even begin to understand or explain Abraham's willingness to obey God at all costs—even the possible cost of his son. Abraham's hope wasn't set on this world or anything in it. Hebrews 11:9-10 tells us, "By faith he made his home in the promised land like a stranger in a foreign country...For he was looking forward to the city with foundations, whose architect and builder is God." Like the old song says, "This world is not my home; I'm just passing through. My treasures are laid up somewhere beyond the blue."[5]

High Expectations

Even as we try our hardest to comprehend faith like Abraham's, we still may be tempted to think, "Yes, but giving up your only son—wasn't that a bit *extreme* of God to expect?" It's actually no less than what he expects from every one of us. We, too, must be willing to sacrifice our most precious treasures.

Here's how Jesus put it: "If you want to be my disciple, you must hate everyone else by comparison—your father and mother, wife and children, brothers and sisters—yes, even your own life. Otherwise, you cannot be my disciple" (Luke 14:26, NEW LIVING TRANSLATION). He went as far as to say, "So you cannot become my disciple without giving up everything you own" (Luke 14:33, NLT).

If you're like many people today, you may wish you could somehow explain away Jesus' hard sayings. But as David Platt warns, we need to be careful not to turn our own ideas of Christ and Christianity into something we're more comfortable with: "A nice, middle-class, American Jesus…who doesn't mind materialism and who would never call us to give away everything we have…A Jesus who brings comfort and prosperity as we live out our Christian spin on the American Dream."[6]

At the very heart of Christianity is a Father who *abandoned* his Son to hang on a cross for us and a Son who *abandoned* the comforts and praise of heaven to *die* on that cross—for us. It only makes sense that the Son would expect nothing less from us than that we abandon all we have for him.

So how do we do it? How do we really desert everything for our Savior? We read statements like this one from Paul: "I press on toward the goal to win the prize for which God has called me heavenward in Christ Jesus" (Philippians 3:14). Reading those words makes our hearts leap inside us, because we really want to be more like our Lord—or sink, because we don't know how to do it. How do we pull this off?

Only by Grace

Grace is God's undeserved favor. We're not only saved by grace; we *live* by grace. God knows we can't succeed on our own. We must have his favor each and every day to guide us and empower us. And the awesome truth is that we *do*! Romans 5:2 tells us that through Christ "we have gained access by faith into this grace in which we now stand." We already stand in God's grace.

As Jerry Bridges explains, "Your worst days are never so bad that you are beyond the *reach* of God's grace. And your best days are never so good that you are beyond the *need* of God's grace."[7]

Paul knew firsthand about God's all-sufficient grace, and it both humbled and motivated him. "For I am the least of the apostles and do not even deserve to be called an apostle, because I persecuted the church of God. But by the grace of God I am what I am, and his grace to me was not without effect. No, I worked harder than all of them—yet not I, but the grace of God that was with me" (1 Corinthians 15:9-10).

You and I can win this race called the Christian life. We can finish well— and we must. We have no excuse, for we are standing in grace.

My Daily Response

Yesterday, you listed your priorities. Today, make a list of your blessings. Write down everything you can think of that you have because of the undeserved favor God has shown you.

Once you've made your list, kneel before God, holding out your hands with your palms facing upward. Say the following prayer aloud, filling in the blank with each possession you listed, "Lord, thank you for _____. It (or he or she) is not mine to keep, but yours to give."

JOURNAL }

My Daily Meditation

The fourth stanza of "The Servant's Creed" on page 6 highlights the tremendous need we have for grace in order to remain faithful and pleasing to God. It should be our heart's cry each and every day for the rest of our days. Please write that stanza below. Then say it aloud as a prayer.

JOURNAL }

[3] Keith Green, "Asleep in the Light," Copyright 1978 Birdwing Music / BMG Songs, Inc./ Ears To Hear.
[4] David Green, *More Than a Hobby* (Nashville: Thomas Nelson, 2005), 7, 195.
[5] "This World Is Not My Home," words and music by J.R. Baxter, Jr.
[6] David Platt, *Radical* (Colorado Springs: Multnomah Books, 2010), 13.
[7] Jerry Bridges, *The Discipline of Grace* (Colorado Springs: NavPress, 1994), 18.

HEAVEN'S PRAISE

Let's begin today by reviewing the first four stanzas of "The Servant's Creed." Please turn to page 6, and read them two or three times to absorb the powerful truths expressed in each verse.

The phrase in the fourth stanza of "The Servant's Creed," "press to win the prize," puts us in mind of a race—and so it should, for that's exactly what Paul had in mind as he said, "I press on toward the goal to win the prize for which God has called me heavenward in Christ Jesus" (Philippians 3:14).

If they are to have a chance of winning, runners must drink plenty of water during a race. That's why, in long-distance races, people with cups of water are stationed along the route. The runners grab and drink so they can stay hydrated.

God designed all of us to need water constantly. Besides oxygen, it's by far the most important nutrient for the human body. People can function for weeks without food, but we need water every day and would die after only a few days without it. And just as our bodies require water each day to thrive, so our souls must have the *living* water.

Read John 4:4-14. In your own words, why was the water Jesus offered so superior to the water in Jacob's well?

Jesus said something very similar in John 6:35 when he declared, "Whoever believes in me will never be thirsty." According to Jesus, our souls *never have to be thirsty again.* His Spirit is a spring of living water welling up inside us. If we continue to drink from that spring, we'll never be miserable, dissatisfied, or without refreshment. And as John Wesley said so well: "If ever that thirst returns, it will be the fault of the man, not the water."[8]

Water for the Thirsty

The Bible tells us that whenever followers of God were thirsty, God gave them something to drink. Here are three examples:

- When the children of Israel had no water in the Desert of Sin, God responded by telling Moses, "Strike the rock, and water will come out of it for the people to drink" (Exodus 17:6).
- After Samson had killed a thousand Philistines with a donkey's jawbone, he was thirsty and cried out to God. At that moment, the Lord "opened up the hollow place in Lehi, and water came out of it" (Judges 15:19).
- When Elijah fled for his life in fear of Jezebel, he was so weary that he lay under a tree and went to sleep. Not once but twice while Elijah was sleeping, an angel brought him a cake of bread and a jar of water to revive him (1 Kings 19:3-7).

The situations we just read about offer three profound truths I want you to see. First, the water came from God—not because the people involved earned it or were good enough to deserve it, but because they were his children, whom he loved.

Think about it. When the children of Israel saw they had no water, rather than being grateful to their God who had never let them down, they grumbled and complained. When Samson was desperately thirsty, he spoke angrily to God, "Must I now die of thirst and fall into the hands of the uncircumcised?" (Judges 15:18). Samson's words suggest that he didn't entirely trust the Lord to provide for him.

And what about Elijah? He didn't even have the willpower to ask for what he needed. Instead, he prayed to God that he might die. But true to God's character, not only did the Lord send all the food and water Elijah needed, he even placed his bread over hot coals to warm it. Talk about over-the-top service!

Isn't it just like God to give us exactly what we need exactly when we need it? Jesus wants to give you what you most desperately need. He wants to commune with you and refresh you *every* day with his presence and peace. He's not waiting for you to become "good enough" or perform well enough; he loves you unconditionally and promises never to leave you or forsake you.

I know Christians who say they're experiencing a "dry time" in their walk with God. They wonder if God has abandoned them. They think maybe God's mad at them for something and has pulled his presence away to punish them. But that's not the God of the Bible. Because of Jesus, Christians can "approach God's throne of grace with confidence"—not because we have our acts together, but "so that we may receive mercy and find grace to help us in our time of need" (Hebrews 4:16).

Thirst Quenchers

The Israelites, Samson, and Elijah had in common a characteristic that leads us to a truth that's simple yet profound. They were all *thirsty*.

Isaiah 55:1 says, "Come, all you who are thirsty, come to the waters; and you who have no money, come, buy and eat! Come, buy wine and milk without money and without cost." The invitation is open to everyone, yet it's limited to everyone…who *thirsts*. Unless one thirsts—really thirsts—he or she won't bother to come to God for relief. As long as we settle for allowing our human knowledge, our possessions, or our relationships with other people and things to fill us up, we're not ready to receive true refreshment from above.

Isaiah 55:1 lists three substances that can quench our thirst and that also represent three needs we all have. First, it says to come to the "waters." Jesus is the Water of Life and our Savior. By coming to him, we find *deliverance*.

Secondly, the verse says to buy wine. Wine often symbolizes joy. When we come to know the Lord, we have unspeakable joy! David said, "You will fill me with joy in your presence, with eternal pleasures at your right hand" (Psalm 16:11b). When we come to the fountain of life, the result is complete satisfaction.

The third element is milk: "Come, buy…milk without money." Milk is essential for our physical growth and development. Peter uses milk as a metaphor for God's Word. "Like newborn babies, crave pure spiritual milk, so that by it you may grow up in your salvation" (1 Peter 2:2). By abiding in Jesus, we receive not only salvation and satisfaction but also *sustenance* to grow every day in our love and understanding of God and in our fellowship with him.

Now those are some awesome reasons to let Jesus quench our thirst!

Thriving in the Desert

There's one more characteristic our three thirsty biblical examples—the Israelites, Samson, and Elijah—had in common: They were unable to refresh themselves. God had to provide the water they so desperately needed.

King David wrote Psalm 63 when he was in the desert of Judah, probably while fleeing his son Absalom and others who wanted to kill him. David didn't stop singing though, just because he was in the wilderness. He composed a new psalm which expressed the weariness and longing of his heart. And he knew only his God could deliver and refresh him in his place of dryness.

Read Psalm 63. As you read, notice how quickly David's prayer turns to praise between verses 2 and 3.

David wasn't able to leave his wilderness surroundings. However, with the Lord's help, he did manage to crawl out of his *spiritual* desert. So can you.

My Daily Response

Let's break Psalm 63 down into simple steps we can follow to help us when our own personal "dry seasons" hit. You may not currently be in a spiritual drought, but this powerful process can still encourage and challenge your faith, even in the best of times. Think and pray through each of these steps as you read on.

Step 1: Take hold of God. David said, "O God, you are my God." We, too, must come to God with live, active faith. Boldly say, "You are *my* God, *my* Savior, who's forgiven my sins and restored me to fellowship with you."

Step 2: Honestly express your desperate thirst and need for God. David said, "earnestly I seek you; I thirst for you, my whole being longs for you" (Psalm 63:1b). Of course, you can't earnestly seek the Lord if you're holding on to sin. Rebellion is a sure way to break communion with God. Confess any known sins to him before moving on to Step 3.

Step 3: Choose to praise God in the midst of your dryness. "Because your love is better than life, my lips will glorify you" (Psalm 63:3). Praise isn't always convenient. Sometimes we're not "in the mood" to thank and adore God. Make the choice to rejoice in your present circumstances.

Step 4: Claim God's satisfaction as you meditate on him. David knew that one-time lip service wasn't enough; he had to stay focused on God—even as he lay on his bed at night. Thank God now for the satisfaction and peace he will bring.

Journal what you just experienced and committed to God.

JOURNAL }

My Daily Meditation

One expression of praise we've not yet explored is dancing. Psalm 149:3 says, "Let them praise his name with dancing." Some denominations frown on dancing, but as long as we dance before God to express our love and joy in knowing him, it can be a wonderful way to praise him.

So go ahead—I *dare* you. Dance now to praise your Lord. Move your feet, and maybe swing your arms! There's no wrong way to do it, as long as it's from your heart. Your body may hate you for it, but your spirit will be encouraged!

JOURNAL }

---

[8] *John Wesley's Notes on the Bible,* John 4:14, http://bible.cc/john/4-14.htm.

HEAVEN'S PRAISE

Through the Hard Times

Today's lesson is unusual because I'm not really the one who'll be teaching it. Instead, I want to introduce you to some friends who've shown me and my family what staying faithful to God through life's storms really looks like. The Beam family—Jason and Courtney and their children, Tucker and his baby sister, Lily—have had a tremendous impact on thousands of people, and I believe their story will impact you as well.

I first met the Beams when I came on staff at The Church at Ross Station, near Birmingham, Alabama, a few years ago. Jason is part of our praise team. I remember talking with Jason at rehearsal one evening and getting my first glimpse into the deep faith of this father.

Jason shared with me about his son, Tucker, who was six at the time. Tucker had cancer when he was only one year old, and he underwent a tough surgery. Doctors removed the entire outer quadriceps muscle from Tucker's right leg, but in time Tucker learned to compensate for the missing muscle. He learned to walk and run. He loved sports and excelled in every one he tried. Jason went on to tell me how thankful they were that Tucker had now been cancer-free for more than five years. That was early in 2007.

Bad News…Again

In February of 2008, at the end of one of our praise-team rehearsals, Jason asked that we pray for Tucker. He'd been complaining that his leg hurt. Jason thought maybe he'd fallen down the stairs and somehow bruised it. I'll never forget the look on Jason's face the following week when he walked into rehearsal. He and Courtney had just heard news they thought they'd never have to hear again—a bone scan revealed that Tucker had a *second* cancer growing in that same leg.

Tucker began chemotherapy the end of February 2008. He had to stay in the hospital three to five days each week, depending on how he reacted to the treatments. Once again, the lives of the Beam family were interrupted by this enemy called cancer. And once again, Tucker had to undergo intensive treatment and excruciating pain.

In May 2008, surgeons successfully removed Tucker's tumor, along with the bone that had been affected, and replaced his bone with a donor bone. By January 2009, Tucker had finished forty long weeks of chemotherapy. For the first time in a year, the Beams didn't have to go to the hospital or clinic for treatments. Tucker was able to return to school and even went out for baseball again (although he was on crutches, so he couldn't run the bases).

When they went for a checkup on January 30, Tucker's scans were all clear. Tucker's words were, "We knocked it right out of the park, and we hit it really hard!" Life seemed to finally be returning to normal for the Beam family.

Tucker's Homecoming

In March 2009, some mysterious blisters appeared on Tucker's feet. This concerned his doctors, so they did CT and bone-marrow scans to be sure all was still clear. A few days later, the Beams received the devastating news that Tucker had developed leukemia. They found themselves fighting yet another battle, this time with an even fiercer type of cancer. It was Tucker's third cancer, and it would be his last.

On May 31, less than three months after his diagnosis, nine-year-old Tucker Beam went home to be with Jesus. During his short life, Tucker touched a lot of other lives. Nearly two thousand people attended his viewing and funeral. They had to hold the service in a high-school gymnasium to accommodate the crowd.

Jason asked our praise team to sing at the funeral. The song he wanted us to start the service with was the Matt Redman song "Blessed Be Your Name." As our praise team walked out and started to play, everyone was frozen in their seats, not sure how they should respond in the midst of such tragedy and grief.

When we got to the bridge of that song, I'll never forget what happened. Jason Beam—Tucker's daddy—stood to his feet and lifted his hands in the air. As loud as he could, he sang, "You give and take away. You give and take away. My heart will choose to say, 'Lord, blessed be Your name.' "[9]

At the end of that amazing service, some forty to fifty people raised their hands, saying they had just prayed to receive Jesus as their Savior—including some of the very doctors and nurses who had treated Tucker!

What We Can Learn

First Peter 1:7 says, "These trials will show that your faith is genuine. It is being tested as fire tests and purifies gold—though your faith is far more precious than mere gold. So when your faith remains strong through many trials, it will bring you much praise and glory and honor on the day when Jesus Christ is revealed to the whole world" (NEW LIVING TRANSLATION). What the Beam family walked through during the past few years has been nothing less than a fiery furnace. And their faith has proven to be genuine.

I want us to notice four qualities the Beams demonstrated throughout their trials. All one has to do is read from their online journal about Tucker to see these qualities again and again. We, too, must have these same characteristics if we are to stay faithful and true through our hard times.

1. Humility. Courtney wrote this journal entry in April of 2008: "God never promised us that this life would be easy. In fact it is downright hard at times. I

often think of a sign that was on the wall of my Sunday school room when I was finishing college. It said, 'If Jesus wore a crown of thorns, why should we expect a crown of roses?' Sometimes when the road gets hard, I want that rose crown. I forget myself and feel like I deserve it. I'm tired and I need a rest. But in reality, I don't deserve anything. James 1:17 says, 'Every good and perfect gift is from above.' The truth is all of the good that happens to any of us is because of Jesus. How can I complain when He has blessed me beyond measure? How could I ask for more?"

Genuine humility keeps us from feeling like victims, as though we deserve more. When we recognize, as the Beams did, that we're utterly desperate for God, that awareness will drive us to our knees and to his Word each and every day.

2. Thankfulness. When we're truly humble, we'll also be thankful. This entry is from Jason in March of 2009, *right after* Tucker had been diagnosed with leukemia: "The Lord has prepared us for this moment in so many ways. I thank God that we were able to even look at some positives today in the midst of all that went on. He is in control. In the midst of the chaos and fear, 'Weeping may last through the night, but joy comes with the morning' (Psalm 30:5 [NLT])."

In preparing to write this lesson, I read 97 pages—nearly 300 entries—in the Beams' online journal, which they started the week they discovered Tucker's second cancer. What struck me most was that there's not even one complaint. In *every* entry, no matter how disheartened they may have been at that moment, the Beams managed to give a word of thanksgiving or praise to their Lord.

3. Praise. Thankfulness always leads us to adoration. Listen to these examples of praise that Jason and Courtney wrote in their journal during the final weeks of Tucker's life: "This is our 2nd Easter in a row to be in the hospital. Even though the location we are celebrating is not where we would choose to be, He is still risen!!!" "With all that cancer has tried to steal and take from our family, the Lord has used it to accomplish more than we could ever imagine. His truth, goodness and holiness are more than we can comprehend here on earth."

Jason and Courtney would not have been able to stand and sing praises to God at Tucker's homecoming service had they not been praising God all along their journey. Praise is a choice we make, because we trust the One we praise.

4. Faith. Shortly after learning of Tucker's leukemia, Jason wrote: "I do not know what is ahead for Tucker and our family. I do know that God is on the throne, and nothing—I mean absolutely nothing—catches him off guard." Perhaps the most incredible statement of faith came from Courtney a few weeks after Tucker's death. She wrote, "While we were at Disney World with Lily last week, I kept thinking about how disappointed Tucker was when we didn't get to take him to Disney earlier this year. Then God gently reminded me that Tucker will never be disappointed by anything ever again, that even the very best experiences Jason and I could have ever given him are nothing compared with what he is experiencing now in heaven. Our best days are *nothing* compared to God's best."

You can read more about Tucker's inspiring story and his family's journey of faith at www.caringbridge.org/visit/tuckerbeam.

Our trials won't be the same as those the Beams experienced. Therefore our faith won't be like theirs. God gives to everyone a measure of faith, depending on what he or she needs. But faith that can move mountains—faith that can get us through the darkest storms of this life—doesn't sprout up overnight. It requires nurturing as we invest time with our Shepherd and obey his commands.

My Daily Response

Among the many Scriptures the Beams clung to during their trials are Joshua 1:9, Psalm 62:5-8, and Psalm 130:5. Carefully read through each of them now. Ask yourself how each passage can help you during hard times. Those times might even be right now.

Please respond to the Lord according to your heart's cry at this moment. If you're going through a difficult time, you may need to kneel where you are and pour your heart out to God in honesty and humility. Or you may want to stand and lift your hands. When you do, sing or say these powerful words to God: "You give and take away. My heart will choose to say, blessed be your name."

JOURNAL }

My Daily Meditation

Write out our meditation passage for this week, Hebrews 12:1-2. This time, *re*write it as a personal prayer from your heart to God.

JOURNAL }

As you go through your day today, look for reasons to offer praise and thanksgiving to God, even in the difficult and frustrating times. Praise God aloud at least *seven* times today (Psalm 119:164). Be sure you praise him at least once to someone else, as you share with that person how good and awesome God is.

---

[9] "Blessed Be Your Name," by Matt and Beth Redman, Copyright © 2002 Thankyou Music.

Through the Dark Times

We live in a world where afflictions and problems are not intrusions into our lives; they *are* life. As much as we may wish and reach for the good life, our days on this earth include a lot of conflict, struggle, and difficult choices.

Ray Stedman wrote, "In God's good order and time, the golden age we all long for will become a reality—but it will take place in the life to come, not in the life of the here and now."[10] Jesus warned us that life would be difficult: "In this world you will have trouble. But take heart! I have overcome the world" (John 16:33).

As we strive to live for Christ, this evil world will despise us. Jesus warned us about that, too. Thus, we can expect two things to happen to us along the way: We'll suffer for our faith, and we'll be tempted to sin and even deny our faith. Thankfully, because of God's grace, we aren't constantly bombarded with persecution and temptations. God knows how much we can bear and won't allow us to be tempted more than we can take (1 Corinthians 10:13). Nonetheless, trouble is unavoidable for each and every follower of Jesus. We can count on it.

Read from Jesus' prayer in John 17:11-18. Why can we expect trouble from the world? How have you discovered this to be true?

So how do we face this trouble? Head on.

Let Your Light Shine

Faced with the inevitable prospect of temptation and tribulation, some Christians look for ways to steer clear of it altogether. An elderly lady once told me that, because the world had become so corrupt, she had kept herself withdrawn from everything and everyone for years! As well meaning as that lady may have been, I believe she was a bit confused.

When Jesus said we're not of this world, he didn't mean we're not to even be *among* the world. In fact, he said, "My prayer is not that you take them out of the world but that you protect them from the evil one" (John 17:15). Jesus never intended for us to withdraw from the people he died for. And Jesus certainly didn't withdraw himself from those who didn't know who he was. On the contrary, he often ate with those people whom the rest of the world called sinners. We, too, are called—commanded—to let Jesus' light shine through us every day, everywhere we go (Matthew 5:16).

When I was in high school, a guy in my geometry class named Jeff wanted me to help him with his homework, so he started coming to my house after school. We became good friends and would go to each other's house occasionally just to hang out. He even started going to church with me. What you need to know about Jeff is that he had no one in his life to point him to Jesus—except me. Although I had little in common with him because he wasn't a Christian, I *chose* to become friends with him.

One of my Christian friends told me how concerned he was that Jeff might have a negative influence on me. I sincerely appreciated my friend's concern. And he had a point—I *could* have easily been drawn away from the Lord during that time. Still, I knew God had given me a strong burden for Jeff and had placed on me the responsibility of sharing my faith with him. Therefore, I asked my Christian friends to pray for Jeff and for me.

One of the most joy-filled days of my life was when Jeff knelt on our kitchen floor and asked Jesus to come into his life. The Lord had allowed me to let my light shine, and I was thankful "the evil one" didn't win the fierce battle for Jeff's soul!

The Prince of This World

The devil hates it when people come to Christ.

Don't just gloss over or shrug your way past that last sentence. Read it again. Stop and think about it before moving on. It's not the final truth, but it's a truth we need to take seriously.

The devil hates it when Christians stand firm on their faith and influence people to come to Christ. His goal is to steal, kill, and destroy us at any cost (John 10:10). First Peter 5:8 says, "Your enemy the devil prowls around like a roaring lion looking for someone to devour."

Satan is the powerful ruler of this cosmos, or world system. First John 5:19 says, "We know that we are children of God, and that the whole world is under the control of the evil one." That explains the persecutions Christians around the world currently experience. For some, being persecuted for their faith is comparatively mild (but still painful)—for example, being passed on for a job promotion or having to sit alone during lunch. For others, persecution is more drastic and may come in the form of physical and mental abuse. During trials of any kind, our resistance to temptation can weaken.

The comedian Flip Wilson once popularized the phrase, "The devil made me do it." A person who doesn't know Jesus can truthfully say those words, since the devil can make him or her do whatever he wants. However, a Christian can't blame Satan when he or she gives in to temptation, as if there were no choice but to give in. As God's children, we're no longer ruled by sin and Satan, "because the one who is in you is greater than the one who is in the world" (1 John 4:4b).

Overcoming Temptation

While the devil is the cause and controller of all the evil in the world, he's not the only source of our temptations. Our own fleshly nature and the world around us can also tempt us to go astray.

Read Ephesians 2:1-3. What have those temptations looked like for you personally? Name them, out loud if possible. Then respond to God. Ask for his help, or thank him for his deliverance (or both).

Whenever we're tempted by the value system of this world, we must have faith in God and his promises to us. First John 5:4 says, "This is the victory that has overcome the world, even our faith." We must believe that God's promises to us and our rewards in heaven are more real and worthwhile than *anything* visible to us here.

When we are tempted by our flesh or human nature—by desires for illicit sexual gratification, for example—then we must *flee* the way Joseph did when he was propositioned by Potiphar's wife (Genesis 39:12). It's no wonder Paul told Timothy to "Flee also youthful lusts" (2 Timothy 2:22a, KING JAMES VERSION).

No matter how much faith we have and no matter how often we flee enticing situations, we'll still be tempted at times. Rogue thoughts may bombard our minds when we least expect them. How often, for example, have you found yourself in church and suddenly battling a lustful or prideful idea right in the midst of worshipping and focusing on the Lord? "Where did *that* come from?" you wonder. Very likely, at moments like those, you're experiencing a direct assault from the devil or one of his demons.

Read James 4:7. What should we do in order to defeat Satan when he comes against us? What's the connection between the two commands here?

Each temptation we face, ultimately, is from Satan. When he attacks, we must fight, but not as the world fights. We need to humble ourselves before God, surrendering our hearts and minds to him. Without God's power and help, we don't stand a chance.

Once you've submitted yourself to the Lord, speak out loud to the devil and say, "In the name of Jesus, get away from me, Satan." That might feel awkward, but what's more important—feelings of embarrassment or your relationship with Jesus? So do what Jesus did in Luke 4 when he was tempted in the wilderness: Quote Scripture that combats the devil's temptation, and focus your mind and heart on the truth of God's Word.

Preparing for War

If we're to "stay right" through the dark times—and every season of our lives—then we must suit up for battle. We need to keep in mind, however, that we're not fighting other people—even if it might seem that way at times! Our foes are much more formidable. "And this is why you need to be head-to-toe in the full armor of God: so you can resist during these evil days and be fully prepared to hold your ground" (Ephesians 6:13, *The Voice*).

There are five defensive pieces listed in Ephesians 6. Each of these is used to protect the soldier in battle: the belt of truth, the breastplate of righteousness, the shoes of peace, the shield of faith, and the helmet of salvation. There is only one offensive weapon—the sword of the Spirit—the Bible. God's Word always prevails. In fact, "the word of God is alive and active" and "sharper than any double-edged sword" (Hebrews 4:12).

Note that there are two areas of our spiritual body—the back and the knees —for which Paul did not list any armor. We are only exposed if we turn our backs and run away from the battle. God has given us everything we need to stand our ground, and we have the *Lord Jesus Christ* to fight our battles *through* us.

Paul also said that we are to "Pray always. Pray in the Spirit" (Ephesians 6:18a, *The Voice*). Perhaps Paul didn't cover the knees with armor because he knew our knees will automatically be protected—as we keep them *bent* in prayer.

My Daily Response

I want to challenge you to "put on" the spiritual armor of God right now. There's no right and wrong way to do it—as long as you do it by faith. This exercise may seem a bit unusual, but it's important to form the habit of putting on the armor every day!

Kneel where you are, and read Ephesians 6:14-17. As you come to each piece of armor, stop to meditate on that piece. Ask the Lord to "fit" you with it now. Ask him to help you better understand what it represents and why it's vital in your daily spiritual battles. Journal what God has shown you today.

JOURNAL

Write our meditation verses, Hebrews 12:1-2. Try to do it from memory.

Now, on a separate piece of paper, write all six stanzas of "The Servant's Creed" (on page 6). Attach the paper to the dashboard of your car or the mirror of your bathroom, and meditate on it throughout the remainder of this study.

[10] Ray C. Stedman, *Spiritual Warfare* (Grand Rapids, MI: Discovery House, 1999), 16.

For this session, you'll need:

- Ice cream—with lots of toppings for everyone
- Books—at least 3 or 4 per person. Make sure they're books that can be dropped on the floor, but try to find heavy ones.

START WELL (10 minutes)

We've come quite a way in our first few sessions, so let's relax a little this week before getting down to business. Go help yourself to a bowl of ice cream—and throw on as many toppings as you want! Once you're loaded up, come back to your seats, and we'll talk.

Give everyone a chance to get a bowl of ice cream and settle back in. Then discuss these questions: → → **1**

So far in our study of *Heaven's Praise* we've talked about thinking right, aiming right, and acting right. Now comes what can be hardest for some—staying right. It's easy to get excited enough to do something good once, but to do it again and again, when maybe it's not so exciting any more, isn't as easy. And it gets even harder when life's throwing its "toppings" your way. So let's talk about how we can not only *act* right but *stay* right.

RUN WELL (25 minutes)

Discuss: → → **2**

I'd like to ask everyone to stand with arms straight out in front, palms up.

If your group is larger than twelve people, have people get into groups of four to six for this activity, and ask a volunteer from each group to help you.

How long do you think you could stand like this before your arms get tired? Allow time for people to respond. **Let's see if this changes things.**

Place a book in each person's hands. Allow about ten seconds for everyone to adjust to the extra weight, and then give everyone another book. Then another. After giving everyone a third book, say:

Some of you may be getting a little tired by now. Others of you are probably deter-mined to see how long you'll last. Those of you who are getting tired, feel free to give your books to someone else—or to more than one person, if you like. As the rest of you get tired, you're welcome to hand off your books to someone else, too.

Allow up to another minute for group members to give away their books. If people are still holding a pile of books after a minute, give them a round of applause, and let those people put their piles of books down. Then have everyone sit down to discuss the following: → → **3**

HEAVEN'S
PRAISE

→ → **1**
- Why did you pick the toppings you did?
- What's going on in your life right now that you wish wasn't so difficult? Where do you wish there were a few less "toppings" piled on?

→ → **2**
- What in this week's readings spoke to you loudest? Why?

→ → **3**
- What do you normally do when you're overwhelmed—unload everything on one person, "share the wealth" with as many people as you can, grin and bear it, something else? Explain your answer.

- When the pressure hits, what's usually the first "God thing" you let drop? Why?

Get into groups of four. Read this week's key passage, Hebrews 12:1-2, and then take ten minutes to discuss these questions: → → 4

Bring everyone back together after ten minutes. Ask for volunteers to share highlights from their discussion time. Then discuss these questions together: → → 5

FINISH WELL (20 minutes)

We've already talked quite a bit about the things that overwhelm and distract us and how we react to those things. But let's look at those "distractions" from a different angle now. Can someone read John 17:9-18? → → 6

Take a minute to reread Dwayne's illustration of the rocks on p. 88. Then we'll discuss. → → 7

Get into pairs. (Pause.) **With your partner, take ten minutes to talk about today's lesson—what hit you the hardest and what God might want you to do about it. Make a commitment to touch base this week to discuss how you're doing. Then close together in prayer, asking Jesus to give you the staying power each of you needs. May God bless you as you walk out your life in him this coming week!**

HEAVEN'S
PRAISE

HEBREWS 12:1-2

→ → **4** • When has keeping your eyes on Jesus helped you "run with perseverance" through a tough time? How did it "perfect" your faith?

• Think again about that experience. What weights are you dealing with right now, and how could the things Jesus has already taught you help?

→ → **5** • Who inspires you to stay in the race and keep running (or to really *start* running it)? Share a little bit about him or her.

• How have you seen some of the things you've learned so far in this study modeled in this group? How has *that* helped keep you running, too?

 ### JOHN 17:9-18

→ → **6** • What are some ways Jesus already helps us to "stay right," according to this passage?

• How can staying in the world, rather than pulling away from it, actually *help* you stay right? Give examples.

→ → **7** • What are your rocks—the true non-negotiables in your life? Where does God *really* fit into that?

• What priorities might need adjusting, so you can not only stay right with God but also stay right with the people he's called you to serve and the things he's called you to do?

DAY 1

Expecting the Inevitable

Most of us cringe a bit inside when someone brings up the subject of death and dying. After all, who really wants to think about death? It's…well, depressing. But we can't talk about "ending right" *without* talking about dying. If you're like me, you're probably wishing we could fast-forward to skip this subject altogether and get to the "good stuff."

And we will. In Week 6, we'll finally have the opportunity to imagine Jesus saying to us, "Well done"! We'll get to discover at last the beauties and joys of heaven, and we'll learn about reigning forever with our King! Now that's the Bible teaching I've been looking forward to ever since we started this study! So let's just jump on over to Week 6 right now. How about it?

Nope. Sorry. We can't skip this week's lessons, just as we can't ignore the reality of our own deaths. Hebrews 9:27 says emphatically that "people are destined to die once, and after that to face judgment." In a sense, this study represents our lives. Unless Jesus returns first, there's no way we can bypass death to get to heaven. We must firmly grasp and live out the teachings of this week to help ensure that we hear praise from our Lord in the *next* life.

Even though death can be the doorway to an awesome eternity beyond our imagination, most people greatly fear and dread the thought of dying. As country singer Loretta Lynn wrote in her song of the same name, "Everybody wants to go to heaven, but nobody wants to die." A character in Ernest Hemingway's novel *For Whom the Bell Tolls* summed up what most people feel: "The world is a fine place…and I hate very much to leave it."[1] God created all living creatures with an instinct for survival, so it's quite natural to want to remain here and avoid death at all costs. I think most Christians can relate to what my friend Scott Dawson has often said: "It's not the *being* dead that scares me. It's the *getting* dead that bothers me!"

What we need, then, is a proper view of death. People who haven't trusted Jesus as Lord and Savior have every reason to fear death. For Christians, however, death is the doorway to eternal life in the presence of Jesus! It is, indeed, the culmination of our service to Jesus.

Paul understood the amazing opportunity death presents to those who know and love the Lord. He knew that by dying he would leave his pain and misery behind forever, and he would finally be free of any possibility of sin. Instead, for all eternity, he'd be with his precious Savior in heaven! Listen to what he wrote as he lay chained in prison: "I eagerly expect and hope that I will in no way be ashamed, but will have sufficient courage so that now as always Christ will be exalted in my body, whether by life or by death. For to me, to live is Christ and to die is gain" (Philippians 1:20-21).

Time Is Short

As Paul wrote these verses inside a dungeon cell, he didn't know exactly when his life on earth would end, but he knew it would be soon. Because of that, he was clearly thinking ahead to the day he would see Jesus face to face.

I heard once about a man who placed a quarter in a jar every Saturday until he reached the age that was the average life expectancy for men in his country. Then he started taking a quarter *out* of the jar each week. When someone asked him why the sudden change, he answered, "Removing a quarter each Saturday reminds me that I'm now on borrowed time."

The sobering fact is, we're all on borrowed time. No one is guaranteed even one more day of living. Actor Michael Landon was only fifty-four when he died of pancreatic cancer. As he faced his own mortality, he made an insightful comment about life: "Somebody should tell us, right at the start of our lives, that we are dying. Then we might live to the limit, every minute of every day…There are only so many tomorrows."[2]

The writer of Psalm 90 understood how brief our lives are. This psalm is one of the most profound passages in the Bible.

Read Psalm 90 now. Notice how long the average lifespan is, according to verse 10. What did the psalmist mean when he said our years quickly pass and then we fly away? How have you seen time fly in your own life? When have you wanted to yell, "Slow down!"?

In my previous book *Pure Praise,* I used an illustration based on Psalm 90. Consider this: If a thousand years is like a twelve-hour day to God—or, as verse 4 says, a "watch in the night"—then how long must our lives be from God's eternal perspective? The average life expectancy of a person in the United States is about seventy-eight years. But when we do the math, we discover that to God, seventy-eight of our years are really only about *fifty-six minutes*! Let that soak in for a moment. Even if you and I live to be a "ripe old age," we'll still be less than one hour old to God. That's less time than it takes some people to mow their grass or drive to work! Talk about humbling and eye-opening!

So, from heaven's viewpoint, how old are you now? To find out how many minutes old you are to God, take a moment and multiply your age by 0.72. Go ahead; I dare you. How do you feel when you consider your real age to God?

Judgment Is Sure

Once we comprehend how brief our time in this world really is, we should want to make the most of every day for God's glory. If the thought of dying soon doesn't quite get our attention, thinking about what lies *beyond* death certainly should. It's called *judgment*. Perhaps the only thing we despise more than the idea of dying is the thought of being judged for something we've done or not done. I've always been amazed that people could actually *volunteer* to have their wrongdoings tried before some celebrity judge on national TV. The last thing I would want is to have my dirty laundry hung out for the world to see!

Yet a day is coming when our deeds and motives will be displayed and reviewed not only by others, but by the supreme Judge himself. Every person—from Adam to the last person to be born on this earth—will stand before the all-knowing and all-powerful God. If you take away only one thing from this study, I pray that the one thing is hearing the Holy Spirit say to you, "Get ready. Judgment's coming."

Read 2 Corinthians 5:1-10. Why do you think Paul said he would rather be "away from the body"? According to verse 10, what motivated Paul to please God, both in life and in death?

Get It Together

King Hezekiah's miraculous healing and the extension of his life is, for me, one of the most fascinating accounts in the Bible.

Read 2 Kings 20:1-6. Notice in verse 1 what Isaiah told Hezekiah he should do.

Hezekiah was very sick. Knowing that Hezekiah's life was about to end, Isaiah gave him some incredibly wise and sound advice. He told him to get his "house in order." Although we may not have the luxury of knowing how long we have left on this earth, we, too, need to get our houses in order. The inevitability of death and judgment before God should motivate us to take care of our personal and public dealings, to make sure they are pleasing to the Lord. And when we consider that Jesus could very well return *today* and take every Christian home, we should find our attention riveted on keeping our lives on the straight and narrow.

There's one more important insight I want you to take from Hezekiah's life. When Hezekiah humbled himself and prayed that God would remember him, the Lord added fifteen years to his life. Up to that point, Hezekiah was the most loyal to God of any king since David (2 Kings 18:5). However, Hezekiah did

some foolish things during those fifteen extra years. For example, he showed his treasures to Babylon, which caused great trouble for Judah in the future. He fathered a son named Manasseh, who became the most wicked king in Judah's history. What's more, Hezekiah seemed to become arrogant—even insolent—in his later years. Second Chronicles 32:25 tells us, "But Hezekiah's heart was proud and he did not respond to the kindness shown him; therefore the Lord's wrath was on him and on Judah and Jerusalem." I know this sounds cold, but I tend to agree with Bible teacher Dr. J. Vernon McGee—maybe Hezekiah *should* have died when his appointed time came.[3]

The moral of Hezekiah's story for us might be this: Before we ask God to give us more days, let's be sure we're willing to use these days for him, to humbly please and serve him—beginning with today.

My Daily Response

The goal of this week is to help you get *your* house in order. So this week, I'll lead you in a step-by-step process to thoroughly inspect your lives. While this personal evaluation may be difficult, I believe it will be one of the most rewarding exercises you've ever done. You'll need more time than normal to complete some of the assignments (especially Day 5). You'll also need a separate notepad or journal this week, so you can expand on what you'll write today in the days the follow.

Let's start today by identifying your roles in life. While you probably wear many hats, hone your list to no more than six or seven major roles. For example, your list of roles might include being a spouse, a student, or an employee.

Write each role in your journal now. Be sure to allow 4 inches of space between each role. You'll use that blank space as you continue this process each day.

JOURNAL

Our meditation passage this week is Jude 1:24-25. Read these powerful verses slowly *three* times. As you do, consider what this passage teaches about ending right.

If you're physically able, kneel humbly before God now. Praise him aloud for the love and mercy he has shown to you. Then ask him to help you apply everything he shows you through his Word about your life and your preparation for death. Commit to God; tell him that you won't let anything or anyone keep you from doing these life-changing lessons this week. Journal your prayer below.

JOURNAL

[1] Ernest Hemingway, *For Whom the Bell Tolls* (New York: Scribner, 1995), 467.

[2] Terrence N. Hill and Steve Chandler, *Two Guys Read the Obituaries* (Bandon, OR: Robert D. Reed, 2006), 7.

[3] *Thru the Bible with J. Vernon McGee* (Nashville: Thomas Nelson, 1983), 349.

HEAVEN'S
PRAISE

Leaving a Legacy

According to the authors of *First Things First,* the desire to leave a legacy is one of the most basic of human needs. It "is our *spiritual* need to have a sense of meaning, purpose, personal congruence, and contribution."[4]

A legacy is whatever you and I will hand down to those we leave behind. It can be something material such as property or a financial inheritance. It can also be memories of our time on earth and our memoirs. However, the most significant legacy we can pass along is not material or personal in nature. It's not money or even fond memories. Rather, it's our enduring influence because we lived out our faith and instilled God's Word into the lives of our children, friends, and others around us.

I recently came across a website where people wrote about the legacies they want to leave. One woman wrote that it was her goal to be known and loved fifty years after she died. A middle-aged man wrote that he hoped someone would speak his name fondly decades after he died. One response that caught my attention was written by a woman who had become a charter member of a small church. She was thrilled to think that her signature would be visible for hundreds of years.

I think each of these well-meaning folks may have missed a much more important point. The goal of our lives should not be that people remember our names, but that they remember *God's* name. In reality, it's of little consequence how extensively we might be known and remembered. Our greatest privilege in life is to make him known. As John the Baptist said, "He must become greater and greater, and I must become less and less" (John 3:30, NEW LIVING TRANSLATION).

Now, that's not to say we shouldn't want to build a good name for ourselves. In fact, "A good name is more desirable than great riches; to be esteemed is better than silver or gold" (Proverbs 22:1). And it's wonderful if others remember us after we're gone—as long as their memories of us serve to point them to Christ and the Cross.

Are you familiar with James Earl Maples? Honestly, I doubt you are. In fact, I'd say few outside his community and church have ever heard of him. James E., as friends and family affectionately called him, was a quiet man—a farmer who valued hard work and simple living. He loved his family, and he especially cherished his wife. When "Miss Virgie" became sick with Alzheimer's in her later years, James E. could no longer take care of her at home. Every day until her death, he spent hours by her side at the local nursing home, making sure they gave her the best of care.

I had the privilege of attending James E.'s funeral the other day. A "home-coming celebration" might be a better name for it. James E. loved his church and his Lord. He trusted Christ as his Savior when he was thirty-eight, and in the forty years thereafter, he faithfully followed God. Everyone who packed the little church to pay their respects knew of his deep faith.

As the pastor gave his eulogy, he told of some humorous moments in James E.'s life, including the time he hand-waxed his new tractor! But the most amazing stories the pastor told were of the many people James E. had personally led to Jesus. Some of them he prayed and talked with for years before they finally said yes. I happened to be sitting next to one of the men he had won to Christ. I couldn't help but notice his chin quiver and a tear well in his eye as the pastor talked. Clearly that man had been personally impacted by James E.'s life—as had everyone in the room.

A Heritage of Worship

Every Christian has the opportunity and responsibility to leave a godly inheritance to those who come after us. And nothing less than wholehearted devotion to God is required to accomplish that goal. Only as we live a life of worship can we hope to make a lasting difference in this world.

We can see in Deuteronomy 6 that, as Moses stood and addressed the Israelites, he understood the tremendous importance of leaving a legacy of faith for the generations who would follow.

Read Deuteronomy 6:1-6. What were the Israelites to pass on to their children, and why? Hold that spot in your Bible; we'll return to it.

The truth and the commandment found in Deuteronomy 6:4-5 are the basis of both the Jewish and Christian religions—that our God is one and that we are to love him completely. Jesus called loving God with our whole heart, soul, and strength "the first and greatest commandment" (Matthew 22:38).

It's important to note that Deuteronomy 6:4-5 also describes the very *essence* of biblical worship. To worship something means we ascribe worth and value to it. So when we love God with everything we have within us, we're actually saying, "God, you alone are worthy to receive all my love, all my attention, all my adoration, and all my obedience." That's what it means to "live a life of worship." Worship is not just something you and I do on Sundays at church. Worship means that "whether you eat or drink or whatever you do, [you] do it all for the glory of God" (1 Corinthians 10:31).

118

Passing the Faith Along

Now, go on and read Deuteronomy 6:7-25. Use a pencil or marker and underline the action verbs (especially the ones found in verses 7-9 and verse 21), that describe *how* we are to pass God's commandments on to our children.

There are some important characteristics we need in order to be sure we leave a legacy that honors God. These are all evident in Deuteronomy 6.

1. First of all, we must be *confident*. I don't mean *self*-confident. I mean that we must have a bold faith in God and in his promises. As you read Moses' instructions, notice how firmly and confidently those Israelites were to present the Lord's commandments to their children. Moses said that when their sons asked them about the laws and decrees, the parents were to tell them of God's mighty works and the reasons for his great commands. Their response was to be clear, without hesitancy or wavering.

2. We can be confident only as we seek to be *like Christ*. In verse 6, Moses said, "These commandments that I give you today are to be *on your hearts*" (italics added). We must *embrace* God's commandments for ourselves. It's not enough for us to merely talk to other people about how they should love the Lord; we need to live a life before others that demonstrates that *we* believe in and worship God from our hearts—twenty-four hours a day, seven days a week.

3. We must also learn to be *content* to spread Jesus' fame, rather than our own. Moses warned the Israelites, "When you eat and are satisfied, be careful that you do not forget the Lord" (Deuteronomy 6:11-12). It's natural to want credit and recognition for what we do, especially when we're feeling unappreciated and overlooked. But we mustn't forget that without Christ we can do nothing (John 15:5). We deserve no glory. It's God who *satisfies* us and works through us—for *his* name's sake, not ours.

4. If people are to take our faith seriously, we must be *consistent* in both our walk and our talk. Moses said, "Be sure to *keep* the commands of the Lord your God." (Deuteronomy 6:17, italics added). That doesn't mean we won't ever sin. I know I make more than my share of mistakes! (Just ask my wife and boys—they see every little flaw I have!) But thank God, he faithfully forgives my failures, and he relentlessly strengthens my areas of weakness. I may never leave a legacy of perfection, but at the least, I want my family and friends to know I never settled for sinful habits and mediocrity!

5. Perhaps the most practical point we can draw from Moses' instruction is that we must be *conscientious* in our efforts to teach our children and those around us. We have to be intentional if we're to disciple others. Look again at the verbs you underlined in Deuteronomy 6. Moses said in verse 7 that we must *impress* God's commandments on our children and then gave us some simple

and effective methods to do just that. One way is to talk often about the Lord in ordinary situations with our families. In fact, Scripture should so saturate our daily lives that it's all around us and even *on* us. For example, I've carried a New Testament in my back pocket since I was in the fifth grade. Lately I've noticed both my boys starting to keep Bibles in their pockets, too. In that one small way, maybe I'm leaving a legacy already.

6. I heard someone say that history never remembers average people; every person who made the history books was extraordinary in some way. That's one more characteristic of people who serve God wholeheartedly: They're *uncommon.* They're not your average, run-of-the-mill Christians. Some are quite young, yet they take Paul's words seriously, "Don't let anyone look down on you because you are young, but set an example for the believers in speech, in conduct, in love, in faith and in purity" (1 Timothy 4:12). Others are "over the hill" by the world's standards. They may even have done serious damage to their reputations earlier in life. But they've claimed God's forgiveness and restoration. Rather than worrying about repairing their own names, they invest whatever time they have left in pointing others to God's great and matchless name.

I have no doubt that "uncommon" Christians who leave an extraordinary legacy of faith will likewise receive some extraordinary praise from Jesus one day.

My Daily Response

Yesterday, I asked you to list your roles in life in a separate notepad or journal. Today, I want you to take some time to plan your own funeral, so to speak. (Yes, you read that right!) Write down what you hope people will say about you at your funeral. If one of your roles is teacher, what would you hope your students say about you? If you're a parent, what do you want your kids to say about you?

This is a crucial step in our evaluation process this week, so please take your time. Try to be as specific and thorough as possible.

JOURNAL

HEAVEN'S
PRAISE

Isaiah 38:19 says, "Only the living can praise you as I do today. Each generation tells of your faithfulness to the next" (NLT). Think about how you can praise God and brag on him in front of someone today. Make sure it's honest and from a worshipping heart, even if you're not having the best of days. When someone asks you how you're doing, you might simply say with a smile, "God loves me, and he's been very good to me, so I'm doing great!"

JOURNAL

WEEK 5 | DAY 2

[4] Stephen R. Covey, A. Roger Merrill, and Rebecca R. Merrill, *First Things First* (New York: Simon & Schuster, 1994), 45.

Fearing God

Everyone's afraid of something. We've all felt our heart rate increase and our muscles tighten when we've encountered certain situations. Common fears include snakes, heights, water, storms, and public speaking.

One particular fear, however, didn't make any of the top 10 lists I found online, and that's the fear of God. God has not always been so low on people's "things to fear" lists. Only a few hundred years ago, Jonathan Edwards delivered one of the sermons God used to shake New England in the 1700s. It was titled "Sinners in the Hands of an Angry God." Even before Edwards finished preaching it, people had gripped the benches in front of them and were screaming for God to save them from impending doom.[5]

Today, if we mention the idea of God's wrath and of fearing him, most people feel we're misrepresenting God and insulting their intelligence. "After all," they say, "everyone knows that God is love. If God loves everybody so much, why should we fear him?" It's certainly and wonderfully true that God loves us. God's love is unconditional and never-ending! However, there are actually more references in Scripture to the anger, fury, and wrath of God than there are to his love and tenderness.[6]

Years ago I wrote a sobering statement in the front of my Bible. I made sure to make it big and bold so I'd notice it often. The sentence was simply this: "Dwayne, you will stand before God someday." Whenever I read that statement, it arrests me and causes me to stop and think a moment about the way I'm living.

My original plan was to include that quote in yesterday's lesson on leaving a legacy. My assumption was that reading that quote would have a similar effect on you and cause you to evaluate your lives. But then it hit me: The reason that the idea of standing before God has always given me such pause and made me "shake in my boots" is my healthy fear of God. I realized that we needed to spend an entire lesson on this essential yet often misunderstood and overlooked attitude.

Defining Fear

Jerry Bridges wrote, "It is impossible to be devoted to God if one's heart is not filled with the fear of God."[7] But what does "the fear of God" look like? I want us to consider a few fears humans can feel toward God. To help us grasp the important differences in these types of fear—and help us discern the kind of fear that increases our devotion to God—let's look closely at two words from the original Greek New Testament.

HEAVEN'S
PRAISE

Phobos: This is the Greek word from which we get our word *phobia.* The word implies flight—something from which we want to run away. The word carries a feeling of dread and terror. One example is when Jesus said, "Do not be afraid of those who kill the body but cannot kill the soul. Rather, be afraid of the One who can destroy both soul and body in hell" (Matthew 10:28). This is the kind of fear and dread we don't have to have toward the Lord—*if* we know Jesus as our *Savior.*

Phobos is the word for fear used in 1 John 4. Read 1 John 4:16-18. What is it that drives out this type of fear and will give us confidence on the day of judgment? What would that look like in your own life?

Literally, the love John spoke of in 1 John 4 is Jesus, who is the *perfect love* we need to give us complete confidence before our Father. Because we place our faith in Jesus, we will be allowed into heaven rather than being eternally separated from God. We don't have to hold on to our salvation—*Jesus* is holding on to *us*! What love and mercy!

While *phobos* can describe the understandable dread and terror felt by people *without* Christ, the word often has a very different meaning when it's used for those who've put their trust in Jesus. It can refer instead to a *reverential* fear of the Lord, which is the healthy and needed fear we all should have toward God. *Vines Complete Expository Dictionary* describes it as "a controlling motive of the life, in matters spiritual and moral…a wholesome dread of displeasing him."[8] A great example of reverential fear is found in Ephesians 5:21. Notice how Paul says it should affect the way we treat each other: "Submit to one another out of *reverence* for Christ" (italics added).

Eulabeia: This Greek noun signifies, first of all, caution and then reverence and godly fear. Thus, this fear is reserved for those who are "godly"—who know God personally.

Perhaps the most powerful (and, I might add, *unnerving*) passage where this word is used is in Hebrews 12. Read Hebrews 12:28-29. What two reasons does the writer give that should lead us to worship God with reverence and awe?

We are presented with two very different word pictures in this passage, both of which point toward holy fear. On the one side, because we are receiving an unshakable kingdom, we should be thankful. Gratitude helps us offer the kind of worship God desires. However, in verse 29, we're confronted with the truth that God is a consuming *fire.* Rather than evoking feelings of gratitude, the image of God as a blazing inferno causes us to cringe in fear and dread.

Isn't that interesting? It would seem, then, that a holy and healthy fear—the kind we should consistently feel toward our Lord—includes both thankfulness *and* dread. But can those two vastly different attitudes really co-exist? I believe the answer is absolutely *yes*—they can and they *must*! We're to be thankful for what God has done for us in saving us and making us his heirs to eternal life; at the same time, we need to be constantly mindful that we'll have to stand before God to be judged "for the good or evil we have done in this earthly body" (2 Corinthians 5:10, NLT).

Reasons to Fear

Judgment is but one motivation for fearing God. There are actually quite a few powerful and more positive reasons to fear God. Check these out:

Fear of God is the beginning of true knowledge. Proverbs 1:7 says, "The fear of the Lord is the foundation of true knowledge, but fools despise wisdom and discipline." Before we can comprehend the attributes of God's love, we must first recognize his authority and majesty. In reality, it is God's justice that defines his mercy. Until we grasp how profound is God's anger toward sin, we can't begin to realize how incredible is his compassion toward us.

Fear of God makes his continued favor possible. Psalm 103:17 puts it this way: "But from everlasting to everlasting the Lord's love is with those who fear him." We can also see this connection in the early church in Acts. The church "enjoyed a time of peace and was strengthened. Living in the fear of the Lord and encouraged by the Holy Spirit, it increased in numbers" (Acts 9:31).

Fear of God is commanded in Scripture. Peter told us simply to "Fear God" (1 Peter 2:17). It doesn't get any more clear and straightforward than that!

Reverent fear leads to holiness and maturity. In Jeremiah, the Lord promises: "I will never stop doing good to them, and I will inspire them to fear me, so that they will never turn away from me" (Jeremiah 32:40). Paul wrote, "Since we have these promises, dear friends, let us purify ourselves from everything that contaminates body and spirit, perfecting holiness out of reverence for God" (2 Corinthians 7:1).

Holy fear was exemplified by Jesus. This is perhaps the strongest reason of all to fear the Lord. Hebrews 5:7 is very clear about the holy reverence Jesus felt for his Father: "During the days of Jesus' life on earth, he offered up prayers and petitions with fervent cries and tears to the one who could save him from death, and he was heard because of his reverent submission."

Nurturing Fear

How can we become good, "God-fearing" folk? The answer is simple: *Gaze on him and be transformed.* As the old saying goes, "Take time to be holy." Make it the priority of your day to invest time with God through his Word and in prayer. No excuses. As you focus on God in personal and private worship, he will show you glimpses of his awesome glory and majesty, and you will learn to fear and adore him like never before. You can count on it.

Here's the bottom line: We can either A) humble ourselves and choose to fear God *now,* or B) be humbled by God's mighty hand and presence when we

come face to face with him one day. If we hope to *end right* and hear God say "well done," we'd be wise to choose option A—for all the days we have left.

My Daily Response

Thus far this week, you've listed your roles and planned your own funeral. Today's assignment is to brainstorm some specific actions you can take now, so that people will speak well of you then.

Let's say you want your co-workers to talk about how kind and thoughtful you were to them. Beside that "wish," you might write that you'll talk to each of them and call them by name every day. If one of your roles is as a spouse, come up with some creative and exciting ways to express your love and appreciation, in both actions and words, to your husband or wife.

JOURNAL

My Daily Meditation

As men of Judah marched toward their enemies, they shouted over and over, "Give thanks to the Lord, for his love endures forever!" (2 Chronicles 20: 21). Boldly shout aloud to God your thanksgiving for his love and mercy—right now. (If it's early, try not to wake up your family and neighbors!) Then ask the Lord to help you to continue to worship and revere him today with the fear that's due him.

Write out the fifth stanza of "The Servant's Creed" on page 6, and say it aloud.

JOURNAL

[5] "Billy Graham audio transcript of Jonathan Edwards' sermon," The Jonathan Edwards Center at Yale University, http://edwards.yale.edu/files/graham-transcript.pdf.

[6] Arthur W. Pink, *The Attributes of God* (Grand Rapids, MI: Baker, 1998), 75.

[7] Jerry Bridges, *The Practice of Godliness* (Colorado Springs: NavPress, 1983), 29.

[8] *Vines Complete Expository Dictionary of Old and New Testament Words,* Merrill F. Unger and William White, Jr., eds. (Nashville: Thomas Nelson, 1996), 230.

Facing God

If you're reading this, congratulations! That means you've made it through some of the most difficult and heavy content in this book—and you're now ready to consider one of the most anticipated yet dreaded events in human history! Or maybe you're *not* ready. Personally, I'd rather do just about anything than have to focus on God's future judgment. But better to face the music now—and discover how we can best prepare—than to be completely caught off guard then.

Let me say right up front that when Christians face God at judgment, it will *not* be to determine whether we go to heaven or hell. That decision was already made by Jesus, when we placed our faith in him as Savior. Jesus took our punishment. Therefore, all the sins we committed before coming to faith in Jesus are forgiven and no longer held against us. We are guaranteed eternal life with God!

Yet, even though we won't face condemnation for our former sins, a day is coming when Christians will be judged for what we've done *since* coming to Jesus. Second Corinthians 5:10 says, "For we must all appear before the judgment seat of Christ so that each of us may receive what is due us for the things done while in the body, whether good or bad."

Because judgment for the Christian is inevitable, I want us to take a sneak peek at what the "judgment seat of Christ" may be like. We can't ask anyone for an eyewitness account, since this judgment hasn't taken place yet, but we can get a pretty good firsthand view through the parable from which we've drawn the major themes of this book.

Read Matthew 25:14-28. Notice the various reactions of the master to each servant when he returned from his journey. Imagine yourself as one of those servants. How would what the master said to you make you feel?

How you might feel would, of course, depend on which servant you were. My prayer as you go through this lesson—and this entire study—is that you'll learn how to be among the servants of Christ who are primarily commended on judgment day.

A Predetermined Event

The first characteristic of the judgment I want you to see in this parable is that the master returned. He went away for a while, but he came back to call for an account of what those servants had done. It's safe to say that he'd planned all along to return.

Likewise, Jesus has already determined he's coming back for his own. And when we realize the judgment that lies ahead for us, it should affect the way we live. John encourages us to "continue in him, so that when he appears we may be confident and unashamed before him at his coming" (1 John 2:28).

A Public Setting

The second clue we can draw from the parable in Matthew 25 is that our judgment will probably have lots of onlookers. Luke's version of the same parable puts it this way: "Then he said to the bystanders, 'Take his mina away from him and give it to the one who has the ten minas.' " (Luke 19:24). Everyone there saw what had happened and heard what the master said to that servant.

Further evidence that the judgment seat of Christ will most likely be public is the meaning of the Greek word for "judgment seat." In the ancient Greco-Roman world, the *bema* seat was a throne where a Roman magistrate sat to administer justice. It was usually erected in some public place, out in the open for all to see.[9] If that's any indication of what it'll be like at the *bema* of *Christ* in heaven, can you imagine the humiliation some could feel? It would almost be too much to bear.

A Personal Encounter

What will make the judgment even more humbling, and difficult, is that we'll be standing face to face with the King of kings himself. We'll look into the eyes of the One who suffered and died so we could be there in heaven at that moment!

When the master in Matthew 25 returned, he addressed the servants not as a group but individually. In fact each of the first two servants had not one but two close encounters of the best kind. First, the master met them to give them their talents. What an amazing, joy-filled moment that must have been! Those servants were no doubt on cloud nine as their master looked them in the eye and blessed them. And for these two servants who remained faithful, their joy was renewed when the master returned and commended them.

There are at least two "meetings" every Christian will have with Jesus—and they're both very intimate and intense. Our first meeting happened when we met him as our Savior. A personal encounter still to come is when we see him at judgment. The question is: Will we be glad to see him, because we lived faithfully for him on earth?

Many believe that our personal lives will be reviewed in detail at the judgment, that something like a video of our good and bad conduct on earth will be visible on a large screen. I'm quite sure this analogy is too simplistic, but it does strike a chord of apprehension, for sure. I don't want the details of my life on display for all to see. The thought of it makes me want to run and hide so the Lord can't find me! (Sound like a certain other Bible story?) Whether we like it or not, "Nothing in all creation is hidden from God's sight. Everything is uncovered and laid bare before the eyes of him to whom we must give account" (Hebrews 4:13).

A Time of Proving

The servants in the parable had been entrusted with some amazing gifts, so it's not surprising that the master inspected their work and rewarded them accordingly. He gave the first two servants more talents, while the lazy servant lost what little he had. In the same way, at judgment, our works on earth will be thoroughly proven or *evaluated* for quality. Some deeds will stand the test; others will not.

Read 1 Corinthians 3:10-15. What building materials does Paul mention in this passage? How will they be tested? What kinds of things do you think equate to each of these materials?

Paul used the analogy of a building to help us understand our responsibility and accountability to God. When we became Christians, the foundation of Christ was placed securely in our hearts, and that foundation assures us of salvation. However, everything we've done, thought, and said since that moment has added to the walls and superstructure of our life. What will matter at judgment is this: Are the works we did able to withstand the test of God's consuming fire?

Think about this for a moment: If each of your deeds went through the fire, what would be left? Erwin Lutzer summed it up this way: "The kind of life we lived would become evident by the size of the fire."[10]

So what should we be building with? How can we know if what we're doing, thinking, and saying qualifies as gold, silver, and costly stones to God? In his book *The Judgment Seat of Christ,* R.T. Kendall gives us five unique qualities of precious metals and gems and suggests how to use these qualities to evaluate each of our deeds.

1. Viability: Will it pass the test of time? Will it still matter to God and others after you're gone?

2. Virtue: Is it excellent? Is it pure? Does it bring glory to God or to man?

3. Visibility: Is it attractive to the spiritual eye? Is it something you would want God to see? Could seeing it help make you or someone else more like Christ?

4. Variety: Does your work for God make a unique contribution to his kingdom? Does it utilize your unique spiritual gifts and makeup?

5. Value: Does it have real worth and importance? Is it useful to God? Is it initiated and directed by him?[11]

Of all these qualities, perhaps the most important is *value.* Paul wanted Timothy to know what was really valuable in life and what he should strive for. Read 2 Timothy 2:20-21 now. How can we become more useful as instruments in God's house?

An Opportunity for Praise

And now finally, some *good* news: God's going to look for anything he can to praise you for! That's right. It's not all gloom and doom. In fact, remember the original "*bema* seat" we talked about earlier? It was used not just as a place to punish people, but also as a place to present awards. Dr. Billy Graham wrote, "When Christians stand before the *bema* of Christ, it is for the purpose of being rewarded according to their works."[12] Keep in mind that we're family! We are adopted into God's family, and Jesus, God's Son, will be our judge. He'll be looking through eyes not of condemnation, but of love.

Now mind you, he'll be fair and without partiality. He won't "let us slide." Nonetheless, you can rest assured that he'll look for every hidden gem and sliver of lasting metal that he can find among our "wood, hay or straw." Paul emphasized this prospect for divine praise when he wrote: "Therefore judge nothing before the appointed time; wait till the Lord comes. He will bring to light what is hidden in darkness and will expose the motives of the heart. At that time *each will receive their praise from God*" (1 Corinthians 4:5, italics added).

My Daily Response

At this point, you've probably written out a rather ambitious list of things you can do to help assure that good things are said about you at your funeral. Now it's time to evaluate those ideas in light of judgment. It's vital that you *scrutinize every goal and activity* to see if it will pass through God's fire.

Look back in our lesson today to the five unique qualities our works should have (page 128). Take the time to consider everything you've written down. Each of your ideas should exhibit at least four of the five qualities. If any don't, think about how you can refocus them. Or you might need to scrap certain ideas altogether. If they *pass,* then put a star beside them, and make them a priority on your to-do list!

JOURNAL

Write out our meditation verse, Jude 1:24-25. Now pray that verse back to God. By the time you get to the last few words of verse 25, you should be saying them loudly and joyfully! Pray them over and over until the truths get deep into your soul.

JOURNAL

[9] R.T. Kendall, *The Judgment Seat of Christ* (Ross-shire, Scotland: Christian Focus, 2004), 14.

[10] *Your Eternal Reward,* Erwin W. Lutzer (Chicago: Moody Press, 1998), 62.

[11] Kendall, *The Judgment Seat of Christ,* 60-61.

[12] Billy Graham, *Facing Death and the Life After* (Waco, TX: Word Books, 1987), 265.

HEAVEN'S
PRAISE

Walking in Forgiveness

This is our final lesson on earth (figuratively speaking—relax!). Can you believe it? This is the last lesson we'll study from an earthly perspective! Next week, our scene will be completely different—you'll imagine standing in the portals of heaven, surrounded by angels, cherubim, and saints of old! Your work on earth will be finished, and you'll even experience a little of what it'll be like to see your Savior face to face!

So how should we end *this* week? After all, it's all about ending right. I've really grappled with this. If you'll roll with my vision above, these are the last words I get to share with you this side of heaven. Therefore, I want to be sure to focus on what I believe will help and encourage you the most. Thus, my question to myself has been: What single truth means more to me than any other? What knowledge brings me more comfort and confidence than anything else?

It didn't take me long to come up with the answer: *I'm forgiven.*

We've talked a lot this week about fearing God and judgment. And those truths are vital to know and embrace as we prepare to meet God. In the end, though, what matters most is that we are loved and our sins are cleansed because of the Cross. The God we fear is also our God who forgives.

Romans 3:23 tells us "all have sinned and fall short of the glory of God." We've all broken God's law. No matter how much we may try to make excuses and point the blame elsewhere, our sin is still *our sin.* We can't free ourselves from guilt.

Enter...the Savior. When Jesus first walked up to John as he was baptizing, John shouted, "Look, the Lamb of God, who takes away the sin of the world!" (John 1:29). Think about that for a moment. If Jesus died to "[take] away the sin of the world," shouldn't the entire world be going to heaven because every sin is forgiven? No, and here's why: Forgiveness has two sides. It must be offered, but it must be *received.* Forgiveness is a gift that's available to anyone, but gifts can be rejected. The Bible is clear that only those who believe in Jesus receive that forgiveness.

So what about the sins we commit as Christians? Are they already forgiven, too? Well, yes and no. Yes, Christ has already died for every sin you and I will ever commit, including those we have yet to do. He's absorbed our punishment, so we can never be condemned—no matter what we do or don't do in the future. Nonetheless, to *receive* forgiveness for wrongdoings after we've come to faith in Jesus, we still have to ask Jesus to cleanse us. Forgiveness remains available to us, but it's not automatic.

Not only is forgiveness accessible to us, it's also *vital* to our spiritual growth. Some might ask: "What's the big deal about sin anyway? If we're Christians and we're going to heaven, why be concerned if we indulge in a few pet sins?" The answer is simple yet profound: Sin breaks our fellowship with God.

Read Isaiah 59:1-2. Notice that Isaiah doesn't say God can't hear; verse 2 says he *won't* hear certain prayers. What keeps God from hearing? When have you been affected by God's "deafness"?

Confession

Our companionship and communion with God are cut off the very moment we sin against him. God is holy; therefore, he can't (and won't) associate himself with sin. God loves his children, yet he hates our sinfulness. God *wants* to fellowship with us, but sin gets in the way. Can there really be a more serious problem than that?

Fortunately, our gracious Master has given us a simple, effective way to reopen the lines of communication and restore our fellowship with him. It's called *confession*. 1 John 1:9 says, "If we confess our sins, he is faithful and just and will forgive us our sins and purify us from all unrighteousness."

There are a couple of powerful truths we need to uncover in that verse. The word *confess* here means to "speak the same thing" or "to agree with."[13] We're to say the *same thing* God does about our sin. That tells us we shouldn't haphazardly throw out whatever sin comes to mind. We should never just make up stuff! We must listen to God and hear what he identifies as sin. Only then can we *agree with* what he says. Also, notice that the word "sins" in 1 John 1:9 is plural. God will point out our sins *individually* and *specifically.* As he does, we must also confess them individually and specifically.

Chastening

Proverbs 28:13 is clear on how God expects us to deal with our sins: "Whoever conceals their sins does not prosper, but the one who confesses and renounces them finds mercy." It's not enough to merely agree with God about our sins; we must be willing to forsake them.

But what happens if we want to hold on to certain sins? Is that an option? Will God just turn his head away and hope we eventually do better? Consider this: How should a loving parent respond to a child who is doing something he or she shouldn't? If the parent really loves that child, will he or she not intervene and take action to discipline that child?

Read Hebrews 12:7-11. According to verse 10, why does God correct us? What does verse 8 say to those whom God *doesn't* discipline?

Did you notice how God's discipline was described? It's *painful.* I've been a Christian for more than forty years; needless to say, I've had my share of good, old-fashioned spankings from God! While some of them—OK, *all* of

132

them—were indeed painful, I can honestly say, I'm thankful for every one of them. Often the inner conviction of the Holy Spirit has been enough to bring me to my knees. You can probably relate to that awful feeling: There's this huge sinking and gnawing down inside your chest that can only be relieved by confession!

I can think of a few times I've been obstinate and tried to ignore God's still, small voice of discipline. During those seasons of rebellion, I've experienced financial struggles, health problems, and other unhappy circumstances as God got my attention and drew me back to him. Like David, I can attest, "Before I was afflicted, I went astray, but now I obey your word" (Psalm 119:67).

Cleansing

I don't know about you, but I hate to feel sweaty and dirty. In fact, anytime I come in from exercising or working in my yard, I immediately head for the shower! I love feeling clean (and I'm sure all those around me appreciate it, too!).

In the same way, we should want to always keep a clean heart before God. Our goal should be to live in a constant state of forgiveness. Notice I didn't say a constant state of *perfection*. We *will* sin on occasion. However, anytime we get "dirty," we should confess it instantly and trust God to cleanse us completely. Remember, neither the Lord nor the world needs to be around "stinking" Christians!

If we're to enjoy clean living every day, we need to embrace two important habits: accountability and self-examination. Being accountable to a person or persons we respect and trust is a powerful deterrent to sin. When you know someone else will be asking you the "tough questions," you think twice before indulging in things you shouldn't. Also, accountability partners encourage and challenge us to grow in our faith and do the things we *should* do. Ecclesiastes 4:12 tells us, "A person standing alone can be attacked and defeated, but two can stand back-to-back and conquer. Three are even better, for a triple-braided cord is not easily broken" (NLT).

It's also vital that we examine ourselves closely. When Paul warned about receiving the Lord's Supper in an unworthy manner, he said: "But if we took care to judge ourselves, then we wouldn't have to worry about being judged by another" (1 Corinthians 11:31, *The Voice*). It's hard to say for sure, but I interpret the verse to mean that, if we confess sins *now,* those sins won't be brought up to us at judgment later. At the very least, the verse certainly implies that we can skip some painful discipline from the Lord in this life!

Either way, Paul is giving us some strong motivation to keep a check on ourselves at all times. We need to "take a bath" regularly, giving God every opportunity to expose and cleanse any sinful thoughts, motives, and attitudes that may be lurking in our minds, as well as words and actions that don't glorify God.

We want to hear God say "Well done!" Today is the day to get ready!

My Daily Response

You'll need to block out 45 to 60 minutes to do this assignment. You'll also need a Bible, and the journal or notepad you've been using this week.

Today, I want you to give your soul a long, cleansing bath by making a thorough list of your *unconfessed* sins. It's vitally important that you meet with God privately, if at all possible, to make this list. You don't want anything to distract you.

Here are the instructions to follow as you make your "cleaning list":

1. Start in prayer. Thank God for giving you this time, and ask him to bind the powers of darkness, which would try to hinder or deceive you.
2. Meditate on Psalm 51, and then pray those verses to God.
3. As you go through the following steps, write only what you've not already confessed in the past. God doesn't remember sins you've confessed, so he won't remind you of those!

   a. Examine your *thoughts and attitudes* before God. Write down any that God reveals to you to as sinful and displeasing to him.
   b. Next, examine the *words you've spoken* to family and friends, as well as to co-workers, schoolmates, or others. Write about any words you've spoken that tore down and dishonored the Lord or others, whether recently or in your past.
   c. Examine your *motives* for the things you do. Which ones are selfish and dishonoring to God?
   d. Now, think about your *actions*. What outward sins is God revealing to you?
   e. Finally, have you *offended* someone, or does someone feel you've offended him or her?

4. Once you've finished your list, read through it, carefully confessing and agreeing with God about each sin.
5. Hold your list up to the Lord. Thank God that every sin is now forgiven! Claim 1 John 1:9 as you pray to him. Ask God to help you forsake each sin and continue to walk in forgiveness. If you've offended someone, ask God to help you go and reconcile with that person (Matthew 5:23-24).

6. Finally, tear your list into tiny pieces, and throw the pieces in the garbage to signify God's forgiveness. God's done with these sins, and now so are you!

My Daily Meditation

Take time during the next couple of days to review "The Servant's Creed." Make it your goal to memorize the entire poem by the end of our study next week. Write a prayer now to God to thank him for what he's shown you this week.

[13] *Vine's Complete Expository Dictionary of Old and New Testament Words,* 120.

For this session, you'll need:

• Nothing. Just *be* there!

START WELL (10 minutes)

Have everyone turn to a partner and take three minutes to discuss this question: →→①

Regain people's attention after three minutes, keeping them in their pairs. Ask for a couple of volunteers to share their responses.

It's important to "get your house in order," isn't it? And you've probably done a lot of work on that, as you worked through this week of *Heaven's Praise*. So let's read the passage that set the tone for all that work you did.

Ask a volunteer to read 2 Kings 20:1-2.

We're going to spend a lot more time today debriefing the journaling you did this week, so let's keep this next discussion brief. But right now, turn back to your partner, and take three more minutes to talk through these questions together: →→②

Regain people's attention after three minutes, again keeping them in their pairs.

I hope you had some aha moments this week as you worked on getting your house in order. You may have also had some difficulties. They might have even been the *same* moments.

The good news is, while *we* may have been surprised by some of our discoveries, God wasn't. And God's with us through this entire process. So let's invite him in now, before going any further.

Stop now and pray for your group as you prepare to debrief this week's reading and journaling. Thank God for what he's already revealed to your group members this week, and ask him to help everyone remain open to whatever he wants to do through today's session.

RUN WELL (30 minutes)

Now, let's dig in. Turn back to your partner, and take five minutes each to share what God's been showing you through your journaling this week and how you've been trying to deal with it. Then discuss these questions; we'll come back together in 15 minutes: →→③

→ → **1** • Think of the messiest home you've ever visited. What upset you most about being there?

→ → **2** • As you've explored "putting your house in order" this week, what "mess" surprised you most?

• Why do you think you weren't as aware of it before?

→ → **3** • What was the most powerful moment or insight you experienced this week?

• How have you responded so far to what God has shown you—or how do you *think* you should respond?

Regain everyone's attention after 15 minutes, keeping people in their pairs. Ask for volunteers to share highlights and insights from their discussion time.

Afterward, ask pairs to pair up so everyone's in a group of four.

As we've explored getting our houses in order this week, we've also looked at one big factor that should motivate us—and it's one that's very often mis-understood. In your groups, read Psalm 90:1-12 and Psalm 103:8-18, and then take 15 minutes to discuss these questions together: → → 4

Bring everyone back together after 15 minutes, and ask for volunteers to share highlights and insights from your discussion time.

FINISH WELL (20 minutes)

We've talked through a lot today, so we're going to end things on a different note than usual.

Ask for a volunteer to read 1 John 1:5-9.

Again, we've taken a lot of time this week to try and process what it will take to end our lives right and what it might take to get our houses in order right *now*. Chances are, if God's been speaking to you through this process, he hasn't stopped talking yet. And even if you do feel you've got a strong sense of what God wants, you probably still have questions and concerns you're struggling with. Wherever you are, we're going to take some time to deal with it right now.

Use the next 10 minutes to take whatever you're dealing with to God. Get up and find a separate part of our meeting area if you need to, but quietly— silently, if possible—pour out your heart to God. Admit to what you're still wrestling with or what you don't think you can actually do but know you need to do. God knows it all anyway, and he wants to give you the answers you need. I'll close us in prayer after 10 minutes.

After 10 minutes, close your group time by reading this week's key verse, Jude 1:24-25. Think of it as a benediction for your group, because it is.

Before breaking up for the evening, talk about how you'll celebrate the end of this study when you next get together. In fact, the celebration will be a part of your next session—so make it count!

HEAVEN'S
PRAISE

PSALM 90:1-12; 103:8-18

→ → 4 • How has your understanding of the fear of God been affected by this week's reading? What's changed? What's been reinforced?

• What wrong ideas about fearing God have you dealt with in the past—or still haven't fully dealt with?

• How can a *healthy* fear of God motivate us to end right? And what does a healthy fear of God look like? Share examples.

WIN RIGHT

DAY 1

Welcome Home

You're here! You made it! What do you think? I know—you're probably speechless. I'm sure I would be, too. Go ahead, take it all in. Feast your eyes on the most incredible beauty you've ever seen, beyond anything you've ever imagined. You're finally home.

Yes, you're in heaven. Did you ever in your wildest dreams imagine anything like it? All you heard and read about heaven in the Bible was—as an old hymn puts it—only a "foretaste of glory divine."[1]

This week is about winning right. As we'll see later this week, there's a sense of "winning" that's dependent on how you lived. However, whatever you did or didn't do on earth isn't important. What's important is that you're standing in this awesome place called heaven. You're not here because you won. All you did was accept God's free invitation. Nonetheless, a battle was waged and won so you could have the opportunity and privilege to live forever. It was no less than the Son of God who fought the battle against Satan for your soul. And as he hung on a cross at Calvary, he became the victor over death and hell when he said, "It is finished" (John 19:30).

Sorry; I realize I'm interrupting. You've just arrived in heaven. Chances are you're preoccupied with someone much more important—the Victor himself! You're seeing your Lord for the very first time face to face. I'll be quiet now and let you savor this moment. After all, there is no one more precious and beautiful and glorious to look upon than Jesus Christ, your Savior and King.

It really is your turn now. Try to imagine what it will be like when you do meet Jesus face to face. What might you do or say? Take the time now to respond to Jesus as though he's here in the room with you (because he is!).

Have you ever heard someone say, "If all there is to do in heaven is worship God, heaven sounds boring"? First of all, that's not all we'll be doing. We'll discover this week that there will be plenty to do and experience in heaven.

But let's assume for a minute that the above assumption is true. What if we *do* spend eternity just worshipping and walking with Jesus? How could anyone think that would be boring? As an old song I used to sing said, "Jesus will be

HEAVEN'S PRAISE

what makes it heaven for me." People who are in love with each other can spend hours and days together and never get tired of being with each other. The more we love God and enjoy talking "long-distance" with him now, the more we'll be thrilled when one day we finally get to be up close and personal with him!

I agree with what Randy Alcorn said in his book *Heaven*. He wrote, "The presence of God is the essence of Heaven...Because God is beautiful beyond measure, if we knew nothing more than that Heaven was God's dwelling place, it would be more than enough."[2]

Paul is a shining example of someone who had his heart set on heaven. Read 2 Corinthians 5:5-8. What seemed to be even more important to Paul than remaining in his body on earth? What was most important about it to him?

Notice that Paul didn't talk about being absent from the body and present with his friends in heaven or even present for the magnificent scenery and activities. Paul simply longed to be present with the Lord.

Paul wasn't the only one to express this heartfelt desire in Scripture. David also yearned above all to be with God. In Psalm 16:11, he prayed, "You make known to me the path of life; you will fill me with joy in your presence, with eternal pleasures at your right hand."

I'm sure you'd love to continue praising Christ and basking in his presence for at least a few thousand years—throughout eternity, in fact—and you'll get to. But first, I'd like to tell you about some other pretty amazing experiences in store for you in your heavenly home.

Learning Your Way Around

First of all, in case you haven't noticed this already, heaven is a real place. Jesus said he was going to prepare a place for us (John 14:2). You're not floating around on some wispy cloud playing a golden harp! Now you can see for yourself that heaven isn't just an ideal or the figment of someone's wild imagination. This place is brimming with more life, activity, and excitement than anywhere you've ever been!

Something else you may have already realized: You're still you! Granted, as you read this, you don't yet have your resurrection body. That will come later, at the resurrection of the just (1 Thessalonians 4:16-17). But even now, you still have your personality (minus the negative and sinful parts, of course).

You still have emotions and feelings, but now they're so much more pure and full of joy! We just read in Psalm 16 how David longed for the exquisite joy he would feel in God's presence in heaven. Erwin Lutzer explained continuing personal feeling this way: "Think of your purest joy on earth; then multiply that many times and you might catch a glimpse of heaven's euphoria."[3]

As elated as you are right now, it may be difficult for you to fathom that for now people may feel heaviness, perhaps even sorrow, in heaven. We can discern the presence of these emotions from John's visions in Revelation 6 and 7. The souls of martyrs under the altar cried out to God, "How long, Sovereign Lord, holy and true, until you judge the inhabitants of the earth and avenge our blood?" (Revelation 6:10). Thankfully, one day soon "God will wipe away every tear from their eyes" (Revelation 7:17).

Not only do you still have emotions, you've also retained a vivid memory. Just as the martyrs under the altar remembered what their murderers had done to them, you'll remember both good times and bad. Paul said, "Now I know in part; then I shall know fully, even as I am fully known" (1 Corinthians 13:12). Of course, only God knows everything, but in heaven Christians will know in the way we've always known—except we'll know so much more.

As you begin to venture across heaven, I have no doubt, you'll immediately recognize people you knew on earth, and you'll know their names! Loved ones, family members, friends who were Christians—you'll not only know them all but be able to embrace them and enjoy their company for all eternity! With the exception of being married, you'll be able to pick up with your loved ones right where you left off! In heaven, you'll *continue to love* and care for those you knew on earth.

Jesus spoke of the continuation of relationships when he told of the rich man who went to hell with his memory intact. Although in torment, the rich man was deeply concerned for his family still on earth. Notice what he said to Abraham when he saw the beggar Lazarus with Abraham on the other side of the "great chasm": "I beg you, father, send Lazarus to my family, for I have five brothers. Let him warn them, so that they will not also come to this place of torment" (Luke 16:27-28). We can gather from this story that death doesn't change what we know or for whom we care.

Perfect at Last!

Dr. Lutzer described heaven as "the earthly life of the believer glorified and perfected."[4] The best news I can give you is that you're finally perfect in every way! In fact, God started you on the pathway to this perfection the day you first became a Christian.

When you first trusted Jesus as your personal Savior, you were saved from the *penalty* of sin—you were *justified*. When you were justified, you immediately became a child of God and a citizen of heaven (Romans 8:16, Philippians 3:20). As you grew in your Christian life, you continued to be saved from the *power* of sin. God helped you become more like him each day through *sanctification*—the process of making you holy. And now in heaven, you have been saved from the

very possibility and presence of sin! The Bible calls this immediate and complete perfection *glorification*. "Those he justified, he also glorified" (Romans 8:30b).

Read Philippians 1:3-6. What was Paul confident about in verse 6? What's your own confidence level about this at the moment? Confess any doubts you might have to God right now. It's OK; he's in the business of making things right. That's what this passage is all about.

I've just got to ask you, how does it feel to be perfect? Oh, I almost forgot that you can't communicate with us; you're in heaven. John MacArthur thinks that the perfected soul "will finally be perfectly free from evil forever. We will never again have a selfish desire or utter useless words. We will never perform another unkind deed or think any sinful thought. We will be…finally able to do that which is absolutely righteous, holy, and perfect before God."[5] When sin is really gone forever, we may want to shout the words of an old spiritual as Martin Luther King did, "Free at last! Free at last! Thank God Almighty; I'm free at last!"[6]

Ushered by Angels

The Bible is our *only* reliable source of information about the hereafter. Fortunately, it's chock-full of glimpses of heaven to help "fire up our imagination and kindle a desire for Heaven in our hearts."[7] And nothing comforts and thrills me more than to imagine how angels will be there to usher Christians home when it's our time to die. Jesus said that when Lazarus died, "the angels carried him to Abraham's side" (Luke 16:22).

In Week 4, I told you about Tucker Beam, the boy in our church who valiantly fought three cancers. In the last days before he died, something extraordinary happened. As his father Jason recalled, "Whenever Tucker would look up he seemed to be focusing in a corner of the room that had nothing in it—nothing, that is, that we could see." In his final hours, he suddenly called out, "No, I can't. I can't." Sensing what might be happening, his mom and dad bent down and spoke softly to him. They told him, "If that's Jesus calling for you, Tuck, it's OK; you can go." A few minutes later, he roused up again. This time he simply whispered toward the ceiling, "How far is it?" Jason said that at that moment, "It made sense to us that he had seen angels." Shortly after that, he passed away.

I can only imagine that when Tucker was carried by the angels into heaven, the first one he saw was his precious Savior, with his arms open wide, saying, "Welcome home, Tuck."

Point your face upward toward God now. Raise your hands as you humbly pour yourself out to him. Worship him from your heart that's being "fired up" now for heaven!

JOURNAL

Our meditation verse for this final week of our study is Philippians 3:14: "I press on to reach the end of the race and receive the heavenly prize for which God, through Christ Jesus, is calling us" (NEW LIVING TRANSLATION). In light of what you've experienced today, write that verse back to God as a prayer from your heart.

JOURNAL

[1] "Blessed Assurance," by Fanny J. Crosby.

[2] Randy Alcorn, *Heaven* (Carol Stream, IL: Tyndale, 2004), 181.

[3] Erwin W. Lutzer, *One Minute After You Die* (Chicago: Moody, 1997), 83-84.

[4] Lutzer, *One Minute After You Die,* 79.

[5] John F. MacArthur, *The Glory of Heaven* (Wheaton, IL: Crossway, 1996), 125.

[6] Martin Luther King Jr., "I Have a Dream" speech delivered August 1963, at the Lincoln Memorial, Washington DC, http://www.americanrhetoric.com/speeches/mlkihaveadream.htm.

[7] Alcorn, *Heaven,* 16.

HEAVEN'S
PRAISE

Relishing Rewards

The idea of looking forward to rewards in heaven bothers some Christians. But did you know that even Jesus had his mind set on a reward? Hebrews 12:2 says, "Let us…[fix] our eyes on Jesus, the pioneer and perfecter of our faith. *For the joy set before him* he endured the cross, scorning its shame, and sat down at the right hand of the throne of God" (italics added).

Paul said, "I press on to reach the end of the race and receive the heavenly prize for which God, through Christ Jesus, is calling us" (Philippians 3:14, NLT). But for some Christians, pressing to win a "prize in the sky" seems a bit overrated, unnecessary, and even kind of wrongheaded. "Since we go to heaven by God's grace with no effort of our own," they reason, "*and* we're automatically made perfect when we arrive there, what's the motivation? Aren't we going to just cast our crowns at Jesus' feet anyway and get on with eternity?"

In case those questions and thoughts have ever lurked in the back of *your* mind, perhaps this hypothetical situation can help you see the answers more clearly:

Imagine you're standing before Jesus at the judgment seat of Christ. Others are probably there watching you as well. The Lord begins reviewing your deeds, including your unconfessed sins, things you did and thought in secret, your attitudes, your accomplishments. This is your "final exam." You may be wishing you could run back to earth for a few days and fix some things you left undone, but that's not possible. This is it—and the results of this exam will follow you for eternity.

The Master seems to be done looking over your works. Now, much to your dismay, he sets them all on fire, while everyone around watches them burn! He's revealing which of your deeds are of high enough quality to endure the flames. He's looking for *anything* he can reward you for. You can't help but wonder what Jesus may be thinking as the fire blazes higher than you had expected or wanted. "That can't be good," you think to yourself. "What will Jesus say to me? Is there still a chance he might say, 'Well done'? He's really taking his time here."

The anticipation is almost more than you can bear. One thing's for sure: The day of reckoning has arrived. This is the day you'll either be rewarded or "suffer loss"—depending on what you did "while in the body, whether good or bad" (1 Corinthians 3:15, 2 Corinthians 5:10). You see, this is the moment you've been waiting for since _____.

You'll have to fill in that blank for yourself. Only you know the answer. Perhaps you've been anticipating the judgment since you first became a Christian, or maybe since you started this study. Or, could it be that your first time to think seriously on what your Savior might say to you was, well, about the time this judgment seat event started? Did you honestly give it much thought as you blew through the days he blessed you with? As you've been awaiting your turn on the "hot seat," did you suddenly wish you'd taken this whole judgment-day thing a bit more seriously?

Wait. He's looking up. He's now gazing directly toward you. Your eyes meet his. Even though this is a time of judgment, you suddenly feel unexpectedly comforted deep inside, because his eyes seem to reveal compassion and deep love for you. (Of course, that only makes you wish even more that you'd never failed him.) His lips finally begin to form a word. He's starting to speak. He says to you…

Sorry to interrupt the flow, but that's as far as our imaginations can take us right now. Thankfully, you aren't standing at the judgment seat of Christ yet. You still have time to invest your minutes and days in loving and serving Jesus more faithfully.

Admittedly, I took some poetic license in writing that scene. I can't know exactly what will happen or how the scene will unfold. What *is* true, though, is that day and that moment will happen at some point in the future for every Christian. You and I both will take our turns before our Master and Brother.

Hearing the Prize

I personally believe the prize Paul had in mind in Philippians 3:14 was to one day hear his Savior, Lord, and dearest friend say to him, "Well done!" It wasn't enough for Paul to merely get his ticket to heaven and then set his eternal life on cruise control, living as he pleased. No, Paul was *determined* to "live a life that is worthy of the calling" God had graciously extended to him (Ephesians 4:1, THE VOICE). I believe Paul longed to *bless his God* by giving Jesus the *opportunity* to commend him at judgment.

Read our anchor parable in Matthew 25:14-30. Pay particular attention to what the master said to the *faithful* servants. What did he invite them both to do?

Notice these words: "Come and share your master's happiness" or, as the New Living Translation puts it, "Let's celebrate together!" The master isn't inviting these servants to come into his kingdom. They were already part of it. Heaven is not a reward that only "special" people receive because they've performed in certain ways. Heaven is a free gift. It's our *inheritance* because we're children of God (Ephesians 2:6).

On the other hand, "the master's happiness" in this case was unique. It apparently only occurred at certain times with certain people. It wasn't a *general* happiness the master felt toward everybody he talked to. He clearly wasn't happy with the lazy, wicked servant, for example. Although all Christians inherit heaven as their eternal, joy-filled home, it seems clear that not every Christian will automatically get to experience this moment of overflowing gladness by Master Jesus. That privilege will be reserved for the "good and faithful."

I believe what will make our Lord *most* joyful is the opportunity to confer his ultimate award of "Well done!" The promise of such opportunities may even have been part of the "joy set before him" that helped Jesus endure the cross (Hebrews 12:2). Wanting Jesus to commend us for our labor doesn't necessarily make us selfish or less "spiritual." It's not primarily for *our* benefit that we should aim at being rewarded—it's for his! And Jesus looks forward to showering us with rewards! So much so that, according to Matthew 25, every time he *does* get to say "Well done!" to someone, he apparently plans to celebrate with him or her—maybe even throw a little party right there on the spot!

Promptings for Praise

God obviously intends to shower praise on those who faithfully praise *him*. He makes that clear over and over in his Word. The main Greek word for "reward" appears no less than twenty-nine times in the New Testament. Several other words—including *crown, prize,* and *boldness*—carry an equivalent meaning. The verses below show but a few of the many qualities and actions the Lord wants to praise us for. Underline the word or words in each verse that have to do with reward.

> Our motives: "He will bring to light what is hidden in darkness and will expose the motives of men's hearts. At that time each will receive his praise from God" (1 Corinthians 4:5b).

> Our good works: "And if anyone gives even a cup of cold water to one of these little ones who is my disciple, truly I tell you, that person will certainly not lose their reward" (Matthew 10:42).

> Praying for our persecutors: "Blessed are you when people insult you, persecute you and falsely say all kinds of evil against you because of me. Rejoice and be glad, because great is your reward in heaven" (Matthew 5:11-12a).

> Compassion on the needy: "But when you give a banquet, invite the poor, the crippled, the lame, the blind, and you will be blessed. Although they cannot repay you, you will be repaid at the resurrection of the righteous" (Luke 14:13-14).

Generous living: "Go, sell your possessions and give to the poor, and you will have treasure in heaven" (Mathew 19:21).

Genuine faith: "Suffering tests your faith which is far more valuable than gold (remember that gold, although it is perishable, is tested by fire) so that, if it is found genuine, you can receive praise, honor and glory when Jesus, the Liberating King, is revealed at last" (1 Peter 1:7, *THE VOICE*).

The Applause of Heaven

The story of Stephen is a perfect example of how God loves to praise his faithful ones. Stephen is one of my heroes in the faith. In fact, I named my firstborn son after him! We don't know anything about Stephen before he was picked by his fellow laymen to help the apostles in Acts 6. Charles Swindoll described him as a "bright flash—suddenly he's there, suddenly he's gone."[8] But it took only two brief chapters in the Bible to solidify Stephen's shining place in the annals of Christian history.

What we do know is that Stephen was "a man full of God's grace and power," and "performed great wonders and miraculous signs among the people" (Acts 6:8). We also know that Stephen remained faithful in the face of severe opposition. Rather than backing down, Stephen stood strong for the Lord he loved and boldly proclaimed the truth to the very people he knew could have him killed. Read Acts 7:51-60. What and whom did Stephen see in verses 55-56?

Did you notice what Jesus was doing as Stephen closed his blistering speech to those religious leaders? While Stephen's executioners gnashed their teeth and loudly growled, Jesus was at the right hand of God, cheering Stephen on! And the King of kings smiled his approval for his faithful servant and brother! Stephen was taking a stand for Jesus, so Jesus "took a stand" for Stephen—with praise from none other than heaven itself!

Do you think Stephen appreciated and needed the Lord's show of approval at that dark moment to help him stand strong? Absolutely. Do you think Jesus relished the chance to *give* Stephen that reward? You can be sure of it. And he looks forward to the day he might get to reward *us* as well!

My Daily Response

Psalm 47:1 challenges us to "Clap your hands, all you nations; shout to God with cries of joy." Even if you're not in the mood, clap your hands to God as you praise and applaud his greatness and goodness to you. Faithfulness to God means praising him in every situation, whether it's convenient or not. Remember, Stephen chose to give praise and honor to God in a situation that's probably a lot more inconvenient than yours.

JOURNAL

My Daily Meditation

Write out the last two stanzas of "The Servant's Creed" on page 6. Say it to yourself over and over to help you internalize the awesome reality of those words.

JOURNAL

[8] Charles Swindoll, *The Living Insights Study Bible* (Grand Rapids, MI: Zondervan, 1996), 1163.

Reigning With Christ

So, you're finally getting your crown—or should I say crowns? Are they tangible—something you can really hold in your hands? If they are, I bet they look magnificent, just like everything else up there! (Oh, I keep forgetting—you can't talk to me and answer my many questions—you're in heaven!) I have no idea which crowns you actually received, but I know the ones that are mentioned in God's Word. There may be more the Bible doesn't include, but here are the ones we know about:

1. *The Crown of Life.* "Blessed is the one who perseveres under trial because, having stood the test, that person will receive the crown of life that the Lord has promised to those who love him" (James 1:12). This reward could be called "the lover's crown." To receive this crown, we must love the Lord more than we love our own life, and we must remain "faithful, even to the point of death" (Revelation 2:10).

2. *The Crown of Mastery.* "Everyone who competes in the games goes into strict training. They do it to get a crown that will not last; but we do it to get a crown that will last forever" (1 Corinthians 9:25). Just as athletes must discipline themselves and constantly train and condition their bodies, so must Christians. Without such determined self-control, we won't receive this reward, this *honor* from Jesus in heaven.

3. *The Crown of Rejoicing.* "After all, what gives us hope and joy, and what will be our proud reward and crown as we stand before our Lord Jesus when he returns? It is you!" (1 Thessalonians 2:19, NLT). Our crowns are more than just some metal crown we hold in our hands when we help people trust Christ as their Savior and when we nurture young Christians in their faith—they become our crown. Proverbs 11:30b says, "the one who is wise saves lives." Oh, that we might have many of these live, walking and talking "crowns" in heaven—people you and I have wisely won to the Lord and discipled!

4. *The Crown of Righteousness.* Read 2 Timothy 4:6-8. Who does Paul say receives this crown?

Every Christian is made righteous before God. In fact, if Jesus hadn't made you right in God's eyes when you first trusted in him, you wouldn't be in heaven right now! This crown is not about making only certain people acceptable to God. Rather, it's reserved for Christians who love the Lord and look especially forward to his return.

5. *The Crown of Glory:* "To the elders among you…Be shepherds of God's flock that is under your care, watching over them…And when the Chief Shepherd

appears, you will receive the crown that will never fade away" (1 Peter 5:1-2, 4). Pastors and church leaders bear a particularly heavy load. I've been privileged to work side by side with many pastors, and I've seen the toll that church ministry can take on them and their families. Jesus will present a wonderful, never-fading reward to every faithful and obedient servant whom he called to be a pastor or elder.

Perhaps the rewards you received are among those we just listed. I hope so. By the way, how did you feel when you received your crowns? Was it what you thought it would be? I can tell you what happens to many Christians on earth when they hear about crowns: They feel guilty even thinking about them. It's as if they think they're not spiritual enough or not really in love with God if they dare hope to win a crown or two in heaven.

But now that you've stood before the King of kings, now that you've looked into his loving eyes and seen the nail marks in his wrists, I'm pretty sure you don't feel that way. I'm betting you're extremely thankful for those crowns, and you know it was worth all your effort and sacrifice to stay faithful to the Lord. Think about it: The more crowns you received, the more glory and praise you can now *give back* to your most worthy and deserving Savior—when you cast them at his feet (Revelation 4:10)!

Have you ever considered why Paul so often referred to rewards as "crowns"? Think about that for a moment. Crowns have always been a recognized icon for ruling and reigning. According to Randy Alcorn, "Because crowns are the primary symbol of ruling, every mention of crowns as rewards is a reference to our ruling with Christ."[9] The Lord wants to crown us, in part, because he wants us to *reign with him.* Speaking of the saints, Revelation 22:5 says, "They will reign for ever and ever." Those are the final words of the final vision of the *final* book in God's revelation to man. What better way to drive home how serious the Lord is about us ruling with him?

Now that you've received (in your imagination) your crowns from Jesus in heaven, think back to what else he may have given you as a reward. Read Matthew 25:14-23. Take note of what the master said he would do for the two servants. Now read the parable in Luke 19:11-19, which is very similar to the one in Matthew 25. Again, notice what the master did to reward their faithfulness. How are those rewards similar to the ones God might give *you*?

The master in Matthew 25 said he would make the faithful servants rulers "over many things" (verse 21, KING JAMES VERSION). In Luke 19, did you notice how the master was more specific? He said he would put them in charge of multiple *cities*. What cities? Are we to assume God wants to set us over real cities at some point in our eternal future? And if so, then where?

The New Earth

I know you're probably still reeling in awe over your new environment in heaven. So you may find it hard to believe that this isn't *nearly* all you have to see and experience! Beyond the Marriage Supper of the Lamb, beyond the Battle of Armageddon and the millennial reign of Christ on earth, beyond Satan and his followers being cast into the lake of fire, there is, as W. A. Criswell described it, "a new, redeemed world. It is to be a paradise regained, an Eden restored, the whole beautiful creation of God remade and rebuilt."[10]

Read Revelation 21. What did John see in his vision? Mark in your Bible every word or phrase that refers to old and new, to things past and present.

Peter tells us that the heavens and earth which exist now will be destroyed by "intense heat" and fire (2 Peter 3:10-12). Much like the flood of Noah's time, this renovating fire will cause the whole fashion of civilized order and culture to pass away. Creation's curse will be gone. However, the new earth should still be somewhat familiar to us, with many of the same kinds of beautiful natural landmarks and formations we love about the earth now.

The new earth will be God's kingdom. It will have cities and nations. Isaiah 9:7 tells us that of the increase of Christ's ever-expanding government and peace, "there will be no end." Many Bible scholars agree the new earth will be a place of growing and thriving culture. I like how Erwin Lutzer describes our activities: "We will most probably continue many of the same kinds of projects we knew on earth. Artists will do art as never before; the scientist just might be invited to continue his or her exploration of God's magnificent creation. The musicians will do music; all of us will continue to learn."[11]

Our Resurrection Bodies

"But how will we be able to do all those things?" you may wonder. The same way Jesus interacted with his disciples on earth after he had risen from the dead—with a resurrected body. Jesus' resurrected body was recognizable as his body—complete with the scars from his crucifixion (see John 20:27). However, it was also a *glorified* body that was somehow able to walk through locked doors and appear anywhere in an instant (see Luke 24:36-37). When Christ returns for his church, we'll receive *our* resurrected and perfected bodies (see 1 Corinthians 15:52). First John 3:2 tells us, "We know that when Christ appears, we shall be like him, for we shall see him as he is."

Imagine a few of the perks that will come with living (and reigning) with your "new and improved" body. You'll be able to travel effortlessly and instantly around the universe! It's likely you'll still enjoy eating food! Luke 24:41-43 tells us that the risen Jesus ate with his disciples. And like Jesus, although you'll no

longer need to eat, you'll probably want to. What's more, you'll get to sit down and talk face to face with Abraham and other famous saints from the Bible (see Matthew 8:11)! Perhaps best of all, your resurrected body will never grow old. You'll no longer know any pain, tears, sorrow, sickness, or death!

Sharing His Throne

While all Christians will receive changed and glorified bodies, we will not all have the same level of responsibilities on the new earth. Every Christian will get to enjoy God's goodness and bask in the radiance of his glory, but we won't all equally "share in his glory" for eternity (Romans 8:17). Revelation 3:21 says, "To the one who is victorious, I will give the right to sit with me on my throne, just as I was victorious and sat down with my Father on his throne." In *Your Eternal Rewards,* Erwin Lutzer expands on this idea, "Almost every time reigning with Christ is mentioned, it is…conditional. Successful suffering, overcoming, and faithfulness are generally…the qualifications."[12]

I realize the idea of reigning on the new earth may seem far-fetched to some. The idea of fallen humans like us laying claim to even a small share of God's throne sounds ludicrous—even blasphemous! And if it were our idea, it would be! But it's not our idea; it's *God's.*

As you stand there in heaven amid indescribable beauty, you already know God does all things well. Just imagine how it will be to reign *with* Christ on the new earth! No wonder Jesus said, "Rejoice and be glad, because great is your reward in heaven" (Matthew 5:12)!

My Daily Response

Our position of authority and the level we'll be rewarded on the new earth will be based largely on our success in two important areas: 1) whether we willingly and joyfully endured trials and temptations for Christ's sake, and 2) whether we humbly served others (see Matthew 20:20-27).

On a scale of 1 to 10, honestly evaluate yourself in those two areas. Journal below why you scored yourself as you did. Then write a prayer to God, asking him to enable you to improve and honor him better through both your suffering and your serving.

JOURNAL

My Daily Meditation

Write out this week's meditation verse, Philippians 3:14, on the back of your business card or a piece of paper. Then put it in a visible place (like on the dashboard of your car or on your desk) and meditate on it throughout your day today.

JOURNAL

[9] Alcorn, *Heaven,* 208.

[10] W. A. Criswell, *Expository Sermons on Revelation* (Grand Rapids, MI: Zondervan, 1966), 105.

[11] Lutzer, *One Minute After You Die,* 85.

[12] Erwin W. Lutzer, *Your Eternal Rewards* (Chicago, IL: Moody, 1998), 151.

HEAVEN'S
PRAISE

Today's study might be thought of more as an experience rather than a lesson. My goal today is not so much to teach you as it is to lead you to encounter God in a deeper and more meaningful way.

Knowledge of God is vital to our faith. That's why we've invested so many hours over the past six weeks discovering and digesting biblical truths. However, it's not enough just to gain knowledge. Peter wrote that we must add "to knowledge, self-control; and to self-control, perseverance; and to perseverance, godliness" (2 Peter 1:6). There's no way we'll hear Jesus say "well done" if we haven't grown in "godliness" and reverence before him.

I know of no better way to develop reverence for the Lord than to encounter him in intimate worship. Focusing all our attention and adoration on God produces in us a transformed mind and character. Paul put it this way: Gaze on him and be "transformed into his image" (2 Corinthians 3:18).

There is no book in the New Testament where upward, vertical worship is more prominent than in Revelation. The book of Revelation makes it clear that "the ultimate exercise of God's people is worship."[13] Not surprisingly, the most powerful worship service recorded in the Bible is also found in this book, in chapters 4 and 5. H.A. Ironside described the passage this way: "Escorted by the beloved apostle John…we are carried far above the shifting scenes of this poor world, and permitted to gaze with awe-struck eyes upon a scene of glory indescribable, and to hear things kept secret from the foundation of the world."[14]

Today we'll get a sneak peek into this indescribable scene. We're going to imagine ourselves standing right there beside John as we watch this service unfold. The awesome truth is that we *will* be there one day.

Are you ready? This is going to be an amazing time of worship! I'll warn you now, though—it may get a little loud. You might want to find a secluded spot where you won't disturb your family or neighbors!

Before we jump in, stop and ask our great God to open your spiritual eyes, so you can grasp what he has in store for those who love him (see 1 Corinthians 2:9-10). Go ahead; voice your prayer for focus and understanding now.

Now let's begin.

The Setting of the Throne

Read Revelation 4:1-6. As you read it, try to imagine the awe and wonder of this sight. Then read it a second time to be sure you've painted the full picture in your mind. What did John see in verse 2, as soon as he walked through heaven's "door"? (Hold this place in your Bible. We'll come back to it again and again.)

It's interesting that John didn't mention anything else that might have been around to catch his attention. He didn't talk about gates of pearl or walls of jasper or streets of gold, which Revelation 21 describes. Instead, as he entered heaven, John only cared to focus in one mesmerizing direction: toward "a throne with someone sitting on it." Of course, the "someone" is almighty God himself, and he's in complete control. J. Vernon McGee describes this heavenly throne as "the universal sovereignty and rulership of God…the general headquarters of this universe."[15] Psalm 11:4 says, "The Lord is in his holy temple; the Lord is on his heavenly throne. He observes everyone on earth; his eyes examine them."

The throne of God is prevalent throughout the book of Revelation. In fact, the word *throne* is used thirty-nine times in the King James Version to refer to God's authority and rule. The clear message from so many references is that *our God reigns*. He's not absent. He's not on vacation. He sits calmly on his throne. And he's not wringing his hands wondering what's going to happen next! No matter how crazy and out of control this world (and our lives) may seem at times, our God is still on his throne, and he's *still* in charge!

When you find it hard to praise, check your perspective. As Jack Taylor wrote, "The perspective of praise is none other than the throne room of the universe where we see God sitting on a throne!…The absence of praise simply means that someone has an inadequate view of God. To know him is to praise him."[16] That's why it's quite natural for the creatures and the people around the throne to worship their God. They see him as he is; therefore, they praise him as they should!

Continuous Praise

Read Revelation 4:6-11. Who are we introduced to in this passage? What are they doing?

The twenty-four elders are the redeemed saints of God. They are his blood-bought people. W.A. Criswell points out, "They are in heaven enthroned around the great central throne of God. They are…seated as God's royal counselors and co-laborers. They have won the victory over this life, and they are crowned with the garland of attainment."[17] Since we have trusted Christ and are part of redeemed mankind, those elders represent us! O the love of God—to honor his undeserving people in such a way!

Little is known about the four living creatures. Scholars offer differing opinion about what they are and what they represent. However, one thing seems certain: Their permanent assignment is to worship God around the throne. Verse 8 states that "Day and night they *never stop saying*: 'Holy, holy, holy…'" (italics added).

The twenty-four elders seem to also constantly worship the Lord. Did you notice how the verbs in verses 9 and 10 are all in the present tense? Whenever—

HEAVEN'S
PRAISE

and as *often* as—the creatures give worship, so do the elders. They appear to lay their crowns at his feet over and over again. So what does this continuous worship mean to us? It means that *right now* in heaven powerful praise is being lifted up to our holy God! And we have the privilege to unite with them in proclaiming God both holy and worthy of our worship!

Reread verses 8-11. This time join the four living creatures and the twenty-four elders when you come to their worship recitations. Speak aloud the entire sentences that begin with "Holy, holy, holy" and "You are worthy, our Lord and God." Beware that Satan might throw all kinds of "reasons" into your mind to try to keep you from participating in this heavenly activity. That's because he hates God and wants to steal all the praise from him that he can. Make the choice, at this moment, to worship God loudly and unashamedly!

The Sighting of the Lamb

Read Revelation 5:1-7 slowly. Savor each moment of this climatic scene.

To appreciate the powerful symbolism of this passage, we need to know something about the seven-sealed scroll. This scroll represents God's purpose and counsel concerning the earth. According to J. Vernon McGee, H.A. Ironside suggests it's "the title deed to this world."[18] Christ created it; he redeemed it, and it belongs to him.

Can you fathom the silence and the suspense as those multitudes around the throne waited to see who would step up and claim this scroll, this title deed to the earth? No wonder John began to weep uncontrollably! "The whole creation has been groaning," Paul said in Romans 8:22, as it awaits redemption—or the recovery—of this legal document. Is there no one who is worthy to open it? No one at all?

Enter Jesus—the Lion *and* the Lamb.

In the words of J. Vernon McGee: "The lion is symbolic of His majesty; the lamb is symbolic of His meekness. As a lion He is a Sovereign; as a lamb He is a Savior. As a lion He is a Judge; as a lamb He is judged."[19]

Responsive Worship

Before you read the reaction of those around the throne, ask yourself how you should respond as you watch the Lamb take that scroll? There stands "the Lamb of God, who takes away the sin of the world!" (John 1:29). The same Lamb who took away your sin.

Now read Revelation 5:7-13. You'll notice there are three different songs in this passage: verses 9-10, 12, and 13. I want you to join each group in saying these words *out loud* with passion in your voice. Imagine you are among those untold millions lifting up praises to the most worthy Lion and Lamb, the King of kings!

Read verses 7-13 *again*. This time say those hymns of praise even louder. God is your audience. He should be your total focus at this moment. You might even raise your hands as you praise him. He is listening and loves to hear and see you worship him! Don't be shy, and don't hold back your praise!

There's one more verse in Revelation 5, and it's key to understanding the attitude we should maintain everyday toward Jesus. Read verse 14 now. Why do you suppose it was the *elders,* rather than the creatures, who "fell down and worshiped"? I'm guessing here, but I can't help but think that it's because those elders—who represent redeemed humans like you and me—had been forgiven much. They had the most reason to be grateful and humbled. Falling down before God was their way of paying *homage* to their Savior and King.

My Daily Response

Kneeling has always been one of the most powerful ways to express praise to God. True biblical worship is the *surrendering* of every part of us to his will and pleasure, and kneeling is the posture of surrender.

Kneel where you are right now. Imagine yourself bowed before the Lamb, as those elders were. Try to stay in that physical position until your heart has had time to mirror your body—in total humility, reverence, and surrender to your King.

When you're done, journal what you've experienced today, so you'll be able to look back on this moment later.

JOURNAL }

Review all six stanzas of "The Servant's Creed." Try to recite them by memory. Which stanza or stanzas hold the most meaning to you? Why? Journal your reasons below.

JOURNAL

WEEK 6 | DAY 4

13. Ray Stedman, "True Worship, Ray C. Stedman Library, http://www.raystedman.org/misc/true.html.
14. H.A. Ironside, *Lectures on the Revelation* (Loizeaux Brothers, 1978), p. 79.
15. *Thru the Bible with J. Vernon McGee, Vol. V* (Nashville: Thomas Nelson, 1983), 930.
16. Jack Taylor, *The Hallelujah Factor* (Broadman, 1983), 24-25.
17. W.A. Criswell, *Expository Sermons on Revelation, Vol. 3* (Zondervan, 1962), 31.
18. *Thru the Bible with J. Vernon McGee, Vol V*, 933.
19. *Thru the Bible with J. Vernon McGee, Vol V*, 936.

Finishing Strong

It's hard to believe we've come to our last lesson. Time has flown by! (Doesn't it always?) This week you've had the opportunity to imagine yourself in the portals of heaven, around the very throne of God. I pray it's been eye-opening and helpful.

I wonder what advice or wisdom those who really *are* in heaven now might impart to us if they could. What might they wish someone could've shared with them while they were still on earth? I've thought a great deal about that, and I think I've come up with a few pointers they'd like to give us.

Look Above

First of all, I can't imagine anyone in heaven who wouldn't say, "It was all worth it." All the toil and struggle, all the pain and persecution, the waiting and wondering what's really in store for us on the other side—now they see it all clearly, from God's eternal perspective. Those in Paradise now know that their light and temporary trials *have* worked out for good. Heaven—and seeing Jesus face to face—makes it all worthwhile! I'm sure they would echo Paul's words that "living means living for Christ, and dying is even better" (Philippians 1:21b, NLT).

Unfortunately, we don't have the luxury of heaven's full point of view. Everything we've staked our lives on, every belief we hold true and dear, is based on faith alone.

And yet, we find that faith is enough. "This is the victory that has overcome the world, even our faith" (1 John 5:4b). The more we focus on heaven and the joy that awaits us at the end of our lives, the more confidence we have to live—and if need be, even die—for Christ on earth. Faith enables us to store up for ourselves "treasures in heaven, where moths and vermin do not destroy, and where thieves do not break in and steal" (Matthew 6:20).

Read Colossians 3:1-3. What reasons does Paul give for setting our minds on heaven?

Look Inside

I believe heaven's residents would also remind us *who* is within us. "For God wanted them to know that the riches and glory of Christ are for you Gentiles, too. And this is the secret: Christ lives in you. This gives you assurance of sharing his glory" (Colossians 1:27, NLT). Did you catch that? We have *assurance*. We have Jesus living inside us, right here, right now. What an encouraging, humbling and thrilling truth! Let's look at a couple of things this awesome reality teaches us.

The fact that Jesus lives in us means we're *forgiven and restored!* We stand complete in Christ. Romans 8:1 tells us, "There is now no condemnation for

those who are in Christ Jesus." So "if God is for us, who can be against us?" (Romans 8:31).

Perhaps you've gone through this entire study with a nagging fear and doubt in the back of your mind. Maybe you've blown it somewhere along the way in your Christian life. You got away from God and quit doing his will for a period of time. Although you've repented and come back to him, still you wonder: "How could he possibly tell me 'well done,' considering all I've done against him?" If you still struggle with such thoughts, let me encourage you to do two things: First, claim God's forgiveness and *forgive yourself.* Second, serve Christ faithfully from here on. As the old saying goes, "Today is the first day of the rest of your life." Make every remaining day count for him. Because of God's mercy and love, you *can* still hear him say "well done"!

Christ living in us also means we can't settle for mediocrity. "For I can do everything through Christ, who gives me strength" (Philippians 4:13, NLT). Think about it: You and I have "the Spirit of him who raised Jesus from the dead" dwelling in us (Romans 8:11). As we offer ourselves to God so he can empower and use us each day, there's no telling what we can accomplish in his name. Jesus said, "Very truly I tell you, whoever believes in me will do the works I have been doing, and they will do even greater things than these, because I am going to the Father" (John 14:12).

My ninth-grade son is on the cross-country team at his school. The other day he shared a thought that hit him during practice. He remembered 1 Corinthians 10:31, which says we are to do everything for God's glory, and suddenly realized that "everything" includes his running. He immediately picked up his pace and gave it his best. Because Christ lives in and through each of us who are his followers, we have no excuse *not* to consistently give our best for his glory.

Look Out

I have no doubt that the saints in heaven would want to both encourage us and *warn* us that Jesus will soon return. Naturally, they would want to echo what Jesus himself has so emphatically said.

👑Turn to Revelation 22. Read verses 6 and 7, and then skip down and read verses 12 and 20. What did the angel, speaking on the Lord's behalf, say over and over?

👑The New Testament writers often wrote of Christ's "appearing," and always conveyed the sense that this could happen at any moment. Here is a sampling of the many passages about his return. Underline the words in each verse below that refer to his coming:

- "For the grace of God has appeared that offers salvation to all people. It teaches us to say 'No' to ungodliness and worldly passions, and to live self-controlled, upright and godly lives in this present age, while we wait for the blessed hope—the appearing of the glory of our great God and Savior, Jesus Christ" (Titus 2:11-13).

- "Be patient, then, brothers and sisters, until the Lord's coming. See how the farmer waits for the land to yield its valuable crop, patiently waiting for the autumn and spring rains. You too, be patient and stand firm, because the Lord's coming is near" (James 5:7-8).
- "The end of all things is near. Therefore be alert and of sober mind so that you may pray" (1 Peter 4:7).

If those God-inspired writers thought his coming was imminent nearly two thousand years ago, then surely we should believe he's even closer to coming now!

Look Around

The real reason for the Lord's delay in returning is not that he's neglected fulfilling his promises, but because he's long-suffering and kind. God doesn't wish "anyone to perish, but for everyone to come to repentance" (2 Peter 3:9b). If those in heaven could shout to us now, surely they would say, "What if Jesus came back today? Look around. Who wouldn't get to come to heaven with you? Who'd be left behind?"

Paul said, "Since, then, we know what it is to fear the Lord, we try to persuade others" (2 Corinthians 5:11a). In context, Paul was talking about his own fear of judgment if he failed to win others to Christ—and understandably so. Imagine standing before the Lamb of God, who was *slain* on a cross so the *whole world* could be saved. Now imagine having to explain why you never told your friend, with whom you spent so much time, about the saving love of Jesus. God said that if they die in their sins, after you didn't "sound the alarm" and warn them, he "will hold the watchman responsible for their deaths" (Ezekiel 33:6, NLT).

That's why we must not forget the most fundamental truth of all: "For God so loved the world that he gave his one and only Son, that whoever believes in him shall not perish but have eternal life" (John 3:16). We can't be satisfied just having private devotion times and going to church each week, although both are important. We must get *outside* the walls of the church and into our community and world.

As opposed to "conventional wisdom," the fact is that the more heavenly minded you and I become, the *more* earthly good we should be. The more we know about heaven and spending eternity with Christ, the more we should want others to be there to share in the joy.

Look to Him

Finally, if the "great cloud of witnesses" in heaven could tell us anything, I believe they would tell us to fix "our eyes on Jesus, the pioneer and perfecter of our faith" (Hebrews 12:2a). Jesus started this work in us. He's going to finish it. Jesus is our redeemer, and he wants to be our source of help and our best friend.

I believe the saints of old would say to us what Jesus' mother said to the servants at the wedding in Cana. She said, "Whatever He says to you, do it" (John 2:5, NEW AMERICAN STANDARD VERSION). The words of John Sammis' hymn "Trust and Obey" ring true: "Trust and obey, for there's no other way to be happy in Jesus, but to trust and obey."

I'm so thankful Jesus keeps it simple for us, aren't you? How refreshing it is that we can boil the success of our lives—and the winning of the heavenly prize—down to one brief sentence: If Jesus says it, then do it.

My Daily Response

Think about people around you who may not know Jesus. Think about your family members, schoolmates or co-workers, neighbors and friends. What about the guy down at the service station or the woman at the cleaners? You've casually greeted them for a long time, but have you ever shared your faith? Write down at least three names of people you'll pray for and try to share about Jesus with them within the next few weeks. This may be the most important exercise you've done in this entire study, so take your time.

{ JOURNAL

My Daily Meditation

In his classic book *The Applause of Heaven*, Max Lucado wrote, "Before you know it, your appointed arrival time will come; you'll…enter the City…You'll hear your name spoken by those who love you. And, maybe, just maybe…the One who would rather die than live without you will remove his pierced hands from his heavenly robe and…applaud."[20]

Bow before your Lord now. Praise him. Thank him for all you've learned and experienced during this study. Then imagine Jesus standing in heaven now, smiling and cheering you on. He is interceding for you, you know. If there's one thing we've discovered, it's that our God loves to bless his children! He is looking forward to saying to you, "Well done!"

{ JOURNAL

---

[20] Max Lucado, *The Applause of Heaven* (Waco, TX: Word, 1999), 194.

For this session, you'll need:

- paper and pen for each person

- roll of tape for each group of 4

- worship plan. If a group member has a musical gift, let him or her use it to lead everyone in song. If not, find a good worship CD, play it, and sing along.

- celebration plan. Build in some extra time if you need to, but get everyone involved. Bring whatever food works—snacks, drinks, desserts, even serious munchie food such as hot wings or barbecue. Decorate your meeting area, too. Celebrate what God's done during your time together—and what he's going to do next!

START WELL (15 minutes)

Have everyone get into a group of four.

We've almost reached the end of our study, but our pursuit of heaven's praise should be just beginning (or going to a whole new level). So we're going to spend time today helping one another process what's next. And afterward, in anticipation of that celebration that's awaiting us in heaven, we'll have a celebration right here! But right now, let's spend some time reflecting on these last six weeks. Take 10 minutes to discuss these questions in your groups: → →1

Regain everyone's attention after 10 minutes, keeping people with their groups. Ask for volunteers to share highlights and insights from their discussion time.

RUN WELL (30 minutes)

Now that we're almost done with this study, let's reflect together: → →2

Ask for a volunteer to read Philippians 3:12-14 and 17. Afterward, give each person a sheet of paper, and give each group a roll of tape. Make sure everyone has something to write with.

HEAVEN'S
PRAISE

→ → **1** • What ideas did you had about heaven, recently or in the distant past, before reading *Heaven's Praise*?

• How have those ideas been changed, or confirmed, as you've worked through this study?

• Now think about that day—and it's not far away—when you can finally hear God say to you, "Well done." How do you imagine that will feel?

→ → **2** • As you've worked through *Heaven's Praise*, what's spoken to you the loudest?

• Why do you think God brought *that* to your attention? What do you think he wants you to do about it?

We're going to explore this race we're in a little differently now. It's been said that the real test of how well we've lived in Jesus will be taken by those who follow us—those whom we've invested our lives in and passed our faith on to. So let's explore together how God might want us to do that.

Let's focus on verse 17 of this passage in Philippians. You might read this and think, "I could *never* say that." It might be modesty, or you could have a really good reason. Either way, let's understand that Jesus has already begun to change us, and that he is making us examples worth following. And right now, we're going to give Jesus some credit for what he's already done.

Use one side of the paper you've been given, and take a couple of minutes to write your answer to this question: *What has Jesus already changed about me that I wish everyone would see?* If you can't think of an answer, write out a favorite Scripture passage or something about what Jesus really means to you. But write something that represents your walk with Jesus.

Give everyone two minutes to write.

Roll up your papers so they look like batons—you *are* in a race, after all. Pass around your roll of tape, and seal your papers so they'll stay batons.

Allow 30 seconds for group members to roll up and seal their batons.

For the next 15 seconds, you'll pass your batons around your group. It doesn't matter which direction you go in; just keep passing them along until I call time. Ready? Go!

Call time after 15 seconds.

Now, open your batons. Look at the messages, and try to guess who wrote what. Once you've figured each other out, take turns sharing why you wrote what you did. Then discuss these questions; we'll come back together in 15 minutes. → →3

Come back together after 15 minutes. Ask for volunteers to share highlights and insights from your discussion time.

FINISH WELL (15 minutes…and beyond)

We're about to wrap up this study. But after we leave, we still have our lives to lead. We want to end our lives right. We want to hear God tell us "Well

HEAVEN'S PRAISE

→ → **3** • In real life, what's hard about passing our faith on to others? How can focusing on what you know Jesus has done for you help make it easier?

• How might others be "getting the message," even when we're not trying to pass it on?

• Who are you passing your faith on to right now? In what ways?

done!" So let's take one more opportunity to consider how to keep pursuing the life God wants for each of us.

Ask for volunteers to read 2 Corinthians 5:1-9 and Colossians 3:1-4, and then discuss: → → 4

Let's close this season in a time of worship. As you do, think of it as warm-up time for eternity.

Lead your group in song.

Let's continue to open our mouths and glorify God for everything he's done and for everything he has yet to do but will. I'll start us off in prayer. As you think of things you need to thank God for, say them out loud, and be thankful for what he's given you to share.

Start your group off in prayer, and take as long as you need to (or can) take together as a group to thank God for all he's done. Then close your study time together by asking God to help each group member experience God's presence and share what God's doing with everyone they meet so that God might say to every one of them…

Well done!

Now let's celebrate!

2 CORINTHIANS 5:1-9; COLOSSIANS 3:1-4

→ → 4 • How would focusing on heaven affect what you do here on earth? Be specific—what exactly would change?

• What—or who—could help you grab and hold on to that heavenly perspective? What one next step can you take to make that happen?

Invite Dwayne Moore
to help you experience
HEAVEN'S
PRAISE Weekly Teaching Videos

Want to make the most of your time in *Heaven's Praise*? Then imagine the author talking with you every week about what you're learning!

Dwayne Moore has recorded powerful weekly teaching videos which highlight the material and will inspire you to keep faithful to the daily devotions in the book.

Leading a small group through *Heaven's Praise*? These 10-minute video sessions work really well to enhance your weekly small group times!